For The Love Of Puppies

Memoir of a Breeder's Husband

BOOKS BY DAN MONTAGUE

Praise for <u>WHITE WINGS</u>.

"The romantic intrigue that flows inside of a mainstream story line is exciting and brilliantly written by Dan Montague."

Harriet Kluasner, *The Midwest Book Review*

"Dan Montague's first novel deserves a wide readership: modern American fiction rarely exhibits such qualities and values."

Ben Martin, *Magazine*, Baton Rouge, LA

"Each resolved mystery reveals yet another more perplexing one, but Matthew and the women of *White Wings* emerge, as does this moving novel, strong, graceful, and resilient."

Publishers Weekly

Praise for <u>SECOND CHANCE</u>

"Montague captivates readers with his second novel, an absorbing story that succeeds in entertaining even while addressing some rather formidable subjects."

Toni Hyde, *Booklist*

"*Second Chance* is a well written romantic novel that builds its premise on love being able to overcome the most nightmarish of childhood traumas."

harrietklausner@bookbrowser.com

"(An) enthralling and old-fashioned romantic novel. The characters are vivid and writing captivating . . . Modern American fiction too rarely exhibits such qualities and values."

Baton Rouge *Advocate*

For The Love Of Puppies

Memoir of a Breeder's Husband

By

Dan Montague

Illustrations by Rob Carpenter

River Bear Publishing

ISBN   0-9779227-0-7

First   Edition

Library of Congress Control Number:
2006904895

Cover design and illustration by Rob
Carpenter

Printed and bound in the United States of
America
by Van Volumes, Ltd.

Published by River Bear Publishing
68 West Main Street
Cummington, Massachusetts   01026

riverbearnewfoundlands.com

Acknowledgments

Acknowledgment for help with this book must go beyond the book itself to those who assisted Zoe and me as we undertook the raising and breeding of Newfoundlands. Jane Thibault of Nashau-Auke Newfoundlnds helped us gain acceptance in the Newfoundland world and often gave her guidance about the building of our kennel and the raising of our dogs. Betty McDonnell of Kilyka Newfoundlands shared co-ownership of our first Newfoundland, Champion Kilyka's Castlepines Jamielee, and unstintingly offered us tips on how best to care for and raise our dogs. Kathy Luce of Dingle Newfoundlands was there for us in emergencies with her guidance and calming good nature. We are indebted to our veterinarian, Doctor Stephen B. Constant, of Westover Animal Clinic, a reproduction specialist, who healed our dogs when needed and helped in the successful breeding of our ladies. And finally, we thank the doctors and staff of Angell Animal Medical Center in Springfield, MA, who have shown loving concern for all our dogs.

The production of this book could not have been accomplished without the computer expertise of our daughter, Melanie Carpenter who spent many hours scanning Rob's illustrations and learning the intricacies of PDF. And we thank our other daughter, Martha Bodine, for her work as copy editor of this book.

And lastly, I acknowledge our grandson, Robert (Rob) Carpenter, for his genius in capturing in his illustrations of our puppies and dogs their sense of humor, playfulness, joy and love better than I could ever do in words.

Dedication

To the memories of Bear, who opened
up a new life for us, and Champion Kilyka's
Castlepines Jamielee, our
first Newfoundland, recipient of the
Newfoundland Club of America's
Register of Merit,
whose love for us never faltered, and to Kelly
Green whose short but valiant life inspired this
book.

Chapter One

Kelly Green

I hold Kelly Green, now less than a pound, against the warmth of my stomach and rub his chest between his front legs. He's the last Newfoundland puppy born of seven and, after twenty-four hours, is fading. He trembles beneath silk smooth fur, his life force trying desperately to take hold of flesh and bone. His tongue, big in contrast to his little mouth, reaches out as if longing for his mother's nipple. But when we place him against her, he's unable to grasp it. Zoe shoots a few drops of Fading Puppy Remedy under his tongue. Kelly Green responds by closing his mouth and pulling back his head. His legs twitch and he coos. I look at Zoe and smile hopefully. Is he coming around? But his legs and paws are still cold, and his head falls back to one side against my stomach.

The birthing of Bess's puppies started the day before, July 3, two days before the due date. We were fairly sure July 5 was the date, which, according to the book, was sixty-three days after impregnation. And what a time we'd had getting Bess pregnant. Twice we tried artificial insemination with semen from champion dogs we thought worthy of her. Both failed. This time we arranged with a kennel to have the sire brought from New York to our vet for a surgical implant. He collected the semen, which he claimed was as heavy as bull's semen, and, opening Bess's abdomen and vaginal track, placed it right next to her ovaries. Thirty days later a sonogram indicated several puppies, and the week before they were due, an X-ray confirmed seven.

At 2:30 on the morning of the third, Bess awakened Zoe and me with her pawing at the sofa in our bedroom. When she headed for the door, we followed her outside. She began digging in the dog yard and roaming restlessly around the perimeter of the fence, a sure indication that she was ready to whelp. Two days before her due date her temperature should have dropped from a normal of 101 to 99 degrees, but it had remained steady at 101. Zoe brought Bess into the house to check her temperature. Bess does not like things shoved up her backend, so I held and rubbed her head while Zoe inserted the thermometer.

Zoe turned to me with a worried frown. "A hundred and two, almost three," she said. "Something's wrong."

As luck would have it, our vet was away on a Fourth of July holiday. What to do? We waited until 6:30, then Zoe called Kathy Luce, another breeder, who was planning to attend a dog show in Springfield that day. Showing a dog means getting up early, and Zoe found Kathy awake and still at home. We were sitting in our family room across the hall from our living room. As Kathy came on the line we heard squealing, like a child or wild animal, coming from the living room. I dashed in. There on the living room rug was a dark lump of squirming puppy and afterbirth.

"Puppy!" I called, and ran back to the family room to snatch the towel Zoe had been carrying around her neck as she followed Bess about the yard. A newborn pup still in its sack is so slippery it can't be picked up without a towel. The head was already free of the sack and the little girl was gurgling for air. As I had learned from a previous litter, I braced her body and head in my hands and swung her downward several times. Zoe said a frantic goodbye to Kathy and dashed into the living room. She put her mouth to the puppy's and sucked out the mucus clogging its breathing passages. I guess I could do that if I had to, but I'm glad to leave it to Zoe. We repeated the swinging downward and the sucking a few more times and finally the puppy cried again and began breathing. Hearing the commotion, our daughter Melanie joined us in the whelping room.

We were somewhat ready for the whelping, having assembled the whelping box in the study off our bedroom, and having brought the accouterments of birthing to the room. But things were still packed in storage boxes. After all, we had two days to go. Melanie tore into the boxes to find the syringe, and Zoe used it to suck out the remaining fluid from the puppy's throat. Melanie then tied a piece of red yarn around its neck. Miss Red, her name until her future owner would name her, was weighed, tipping the scales at one pound. No bigger than a little red squirrel, we placed her in a box near her one hundred and thirty pound mom. It was too early for nursing, but Bess gave her a thorough bath with her tongue.

Twenty-five minutes later, Bess raised her great black tail, and out slipped another puppy. Using a towel we picked up a squirming sack and its afterbirth, liberated the puppy's head from the sack and sucked out the fluid until it was breathing. Mr. Orange weighed one and a half pounds.

So it continued until 10:07 when the sixth puppy was born. By this time we were placing the babies next to their mom, squeezing milk from her nipples and rubbing it against the puppies' mouths. Their little heads bobbed against the nipple as if they thought this was pretty nice, but still they didn't get the idea. All of them were black with heads and noses that held the promise of beautiful Newfoundland faces. Tiny ears were twisted closed and their eyes were days from opening. But their noses were in good working condition and they sniffed and sniffed for their mom. Squirming about next to her, they began a lullaby of cooing and gentle sighing interrupted occasionally by a yip or a snuffle.

We stood by or sat on the edge of the whelping box and waited for number seven. The vet had been certain he'd seen one more head and vertebrae in the X-ray. When an hour and a half had passed, Melanie said she thought it was time to induce contractions. If there was a puppy in her, it had to be extracted, dead or alive, for the health of the mother. Our daughter administered a shot of oxytosin beneath the skin between Bess's shoulders. Minutes later, Bess got up and went to the dog yard. I followed her around with a towel at the ready just in case. And sure enough she squatted and produced another puppy. I snatched it up from the ground, holding it while Zoe tried to free its head from the sack. Meanwhile, Bess was lunging for the afterbirth which instinct instructs her to consume. She got hold of it and tried to tug it and the sack still containing the puppy out of our hands. We were afraid she'd tear the umbilical cord from the puppy's body. I grabbed the afterbirth out of her mouth, cutting the cord with my thumb nail. Meanwhile, Zoe was struggling with the slippery sack still wrapped around the head. Finally she managed to insert a finger into the sack and tear it open, pulling it away from the puppy's head. She sucked fluid from its mouth, then I rushed the puppy upstairs, rubbing its chest between its front legs vigorously with the towel. I tried swinging it down to clear its breathing while Melanie searched for the syringe to remove mucus from its throat. Somehow we had misplaced the syringe and Zoe and I, tired from lack of sleep and terrified for puppy seven, got frantic. Melanie calmed us down, and Zoe resorted to using her own mouth to clear the puppy's throat. Eventually, the puppy began gasping for air and uttered a faint cry.

But something was wrong. He was very limp, and as he gasped for air, bubbles oozed from his nose. We decided to call Kathy again, this time finding her already at the dog show in Springfield. Zoe explained the situation to Kathy. "You're gonna laugh at this and think I'm crazy," Kathy said, lightening our mood with one of her legendary laughs. "Hold the puppy firmly high above your head and then bend over quickly bringing him all the way down between your legs. It looks weird, but do it anyway. Do it three or four times and repeat if you need to. It might help."

I did as she said, alternating this windmilling procedure with rubbing his chest with the towel. We continued rubbing and shaking his little body down for forty-five minutes. Only then did the bubbles in his nose stop. The little guy made some cooing sounds and started nursing. It was a time for rejoicing. Together we had pulled him through to life from the very edge of dying. Our grandson McKey had joined us and chose a piece of yarn that was kelly green to tie around his neck. "This little fella has the luck of the Irish," he said. "Let's call him Kelly Green."

The balance of Saturday afternoon, Zoe stayed with Bess and her new family while Melanie managed to take care of the house and produce dinner. I took our other four Newfoundland ladies for walks two at a time. They knew something was up and were anxious. Jamie, grandmother to the new puppies, was most upset because her purpose in life is to be Zoe's shadow. But Zoe was busy with the puppies. Ellie, whom we had bred unsuccessfully the same day as Bess, wondered why Bess had the puppies and she didn't. Ellie's daughter, Patsy, was so excited about the whole event that she decided to go into heat.

And Waltzing Mathilda, still only year old, was just plain anxious to go for a walk. They all needed attention and I needed to get out of the house for a while. When I met our neighbors, I told them about Kelly Green and how we had pulled him through after almost losing him. They shared our joy.

That night I took the first watch from six to midnight. Zoe slept on a futon in Melanie's workroom across the upstairs hall. I stayed awake with television movies. When the puppies squealed, I put Bess in the whelping box. The box is five foot square with two foot sides, plenty of room for Bess and her puppies. A heating pad in one corner and a light shining in the other tended to attract the puppies to their warmth. But the minute they smelled the presence of their mom, they began swimming across the blanketed floor of the box. Out went their front legs, breast stroke style, pulling them in what they knew was their mother's direction. A first time mother, Bess didn't seem to know what to make of this squirming mass of puppies, so we had to be very careful she didn't place her big paw, with her hundred and thirty pounds behind it, on a puppy's back. For six hours that was my job.

At midnight, Zoe took over and I stumbled into bed on the futon, immediately falling asleep. About three in the morning I got up to go the bathroom. Zoe was there, holding Kelly Green. "We've got a problem," she said. "He's not nursing and he's very weak." She gave him to me and I rubbed his limp little body. She filled a hot water bottle, and I lay in bed with the bottle on my stomach and Kelly Green pressed against it. His mouth opened and his tongue came out, wanting, pleading for something. Using an eyedropper, Zoe gave him some more of the homeopathic remedy for what is called Fading Puppy Syndrome. He quivered, wiggled his little cold legs and sighed.

I continue to hold Kelly Green against my stomach. Inside his little body the life force moves through veins and tissues, trying to keep the heart and lungs working. As he lies against me, occasionally twitching his cold little legs, he looks at me through closed eyes and sighs a plaintive plea for help. Again and again we try to windmill life back into him, and still he struggles for air. We realize that his tongue, as it curves out of his mouth, is not asking for milk. He's trying to breath.

How many times, in a former life as a parish priest, was I at the bedside of the dying. I've watched a father, or mother, or husband, or child fade away as this essence that makes the

17

difference between being alive and not alive faded from their bodies. I think of this as I hold Kelly Green. When parishioners stood beside me as their loved ones died, I had to comfort them with words that transcended the finality of death. "His pain is over now," I might say. "She is with God in heaven," basically words from the Episcopal Prayer Book and the tradition of two thousand years. But as I looked into the eyes of the wife or husband or mother or father, they looked back with anger. "Tell me," they demanded, "why did she die? Why did God take him?" My answers were inadequate. Now, thirty years later, I'm not required to give answers. I have no answers.

All I have is Kelly Green lying on my stomach, panting to stay alive.

Melanie offers to relieve me and I pass the puppy to her. For twenty minutes she warms him against her stomach and rubs his body. Then she looks up at us and says, "He's gone." The room falls silent. Even the puppies seem to stop cooing. Or do I imagine it? Zoe and I come to the bed where Melanie is lying with Kelly Green, his head limp against her. There's no twitching of his legs, no plaintive sigh for help. Only bubbles coming from his nose.

"Do you want me to . . .?" I say to Zoe.

"No," she says adamantly with the anger

that flails out at death. "I'll take care of it." She leaves with Kelly Green. Melanie goes with her.

I tend to the other puppies. Zoe and Melanie haven't been gone two minutes before Bess realizes one of her puppies is missing. She rises up from the other six and stares down at them as if counting. Then she leaves the box and begins searching the room and the hall and Melanie's workroom where the futon is. She looks under beds, in corners and behind doors, racing through rooms. She rips all the cushions off the sofa in the bedroom and digs into the crevices. I don't try to stop her. I can't believe dogs can count, so what alerted her? Whatever mystery of nature it was, Bess knows that Kelly Green is gone and she must find him. Even hours later, she makes the rounds looking for her puppy. When she comes back to the whelping box, I take her big head in my arms and hold my face next to hers. "I'm sorry Bess. Your baby's gone." She doesn't ask why or where? She isn't angry. She simply wants Kelly Green back.

When Zoe and Melanie return, I learn that Zoe wrapped Kelly Green in her Harry Potter shawl. Then Melanie took him to our orchard above the river and buried him. In the bedroom with Bess at our side, we hold each other and weep.

"He tried so hard to live," I say. "So hard."

Melanie buried him next to the grave of Bear who, we decided, will take care of him. Bear died at age thirteen the previous year. He was a Lab-Newfoundland mix which we'd gotten from the Boston Animal Rescue League when he was two.

If anyone can take care of Kelly Green, it's old Bear. He took care of us for eleven years and pulled us through some tough times as Zoe and I entered retirement. It was Bear's kindness and inspiration that led us to our new career raising Newfoundlands. And it was our desire to raise Newfoundlands that led us to a two hundred year old house in western Massachusetts located on the banks of the Westfield River.

Chapter Two

Bear

*I*n 1992, two years before I retired, the trip home from my office in Boston seemed to take longer and longer — forty-five minutes if I was lucky with traffic. When I pulled up in front of our house, Zoe met me at the door.

"Get back in the car," she said. "I want to show you something."

"Where're we going?"

"To the Boston Animal Rescue League." In the car she continued. "We don't have to get him if you don't like him, but I want you to meet him."

"A dog?"

"Yes."

"I didn't know we were looking for a dog," I said guardedly. I could tell from Zoe's enthusiasm that I was facing a *fait accompli.*

"Well, I was just walking through their kennels looking at dogs and this one picked me out."

"He picked you out?"

"Yes. They say he's a Lab and Newfoundland mix, all black except for a white patch on his chest."

"How big?"

"He's just right."

The attendant led us past several sad-eyed

dogs longing for an owner, and down to the cage of an enormous Lab. The dog leaped at the gate to greet Zoe. "You were here earlier," the attendant said to Zoe. "Would you like to take him for a walk around the yard?" Zoe beamed and took the leash from the attendant. "His name is Bear," the young woman said as she led us to the yard. He was as big as a Newfoundland but looked exactly like a Labrador. Bear seemed to know where the yard was, because he tugged Zoe toward the door.

Once outside, she walked him around the perimeter of the fence. Every ten feet or so she stopped to rub his head and whisper something in his ear. Completing the circle, she asked, "Want to take him around?"

"Sure." First we walked and then we ran, Bear dancing at the end of his leash like a puppy. Pulling up beside Zoe, I took his head in my hands and looked into his eyes. "I want to go home with you," his eyes said. I nodded. "I think we've got a dog," I said to Zoe.

We couldn't take him home that day because he had to be neutered. In the car I asked Zoe what she had whispered in Bear's ear. "I told him to tell you that he wants to live with us."

The previous summer we had moved from a small two bedroom condo in Boston into a three story house on Gregory Street in Marblehead, Massachusetts. We needed extra room for our daughter Melanie and her two boys after her health had failed and her marriage ended. At first the doctors diagnosed her illness as laziness, then called it depression, then Chronic Fatigue Syndrome. Later, when medical science caught up with the reality of her particular virus, it was diagnosed as Hepatitis C which had been working its way clandestinely into her liver after a blood transfusion some years earlier.

The next day we brought Bear home. He wore a stiff plastic collar and looked like an Elizabethan gentleman, but it kept him from licking the tender spot through which the vet had extracted his maleness. He banged around the house knocking into things with his collar, but seemed to like what he saw. The backyard was fenced, so he was free to roam the yard by himself. That night he slept in our bedroom on a love seat at the end of our bed, staking claim to it as his spot for all future nights.

Marblehead is situated on the ocean and has a huge harbor sheltered by a peninsula called the Neck. Hundreds of sailing boats and yachts anchor there making the town the sailing capital of the east coast. In 1812 Old Ironsides sought shelter there when it was pursued by three British frigates. As the British approached the mouth of the harbor, cannons from Fort Sewall opened fire and drove them off.

Bear loved the harbor, especially on hot summer days. Two blocks from our house was a small yacht club located next to the lobster boat pier. Bear would climb down the rocks to the water and swim out to the lobster boats after they'd docked, and around the sail boats at the yacht club. When it was time to go, I would call him to come. He'd look at me with this blank expression as if he had no idea who I was. When I waded into the water to get him, he'd swim out into the deep water. One day, after I managed to get stranded on some slippery rocks, he beat me back to the rock steps and dashed to the top. By the time I got out of the water and up the steps, Bear had gone into the back door of the yacht club and was helping himself to a luncheon buffet. He was such a big dog that club members dared to do little more than yell at him. When he'd eaten all he wanted, he shook the harbor water from his back onto the buffet table and left.

Bear's blank look disguised an active sense of humor. At the end of the harbor where a causeway connected the mainland with the Neck, there was a large, sandy beach on the ocean side. Dogs were not permitted on this beach during the summer. On the harbor side was Dog Beach, so declared by the dog owners of the town. Here Bear cavorted with other dogs up and down the beach and in the water. He took special delight in using his long legs to bound through the shallow water stealing tennis balls thrown to other dogs. When I would try to retrieve the balls for their lawful owners, he'd saunter out into deep water and give me his look: "Do I know you?" Only a dog treat would get him to shore. As he gobbled it up, I swear he was smiling.

Now that we had Bear, I thought it was great that Zoe wanted a dog. What I was beginning to realize was how much having Bear meant to her. The previous year had been especially hard for Zoe. The hour and half commute each way to her job as a project manager for Digital Equipment Corporation, along with the responsibilities of being a manager, were a strain both physically and emotionally. Then, in November, while leading a training conference, she had come down with pneumonia which left her severely debilitated. And at home our way of life had changed dramatically. Instead of just the two of us living in Boston close to its theaters and restaurants and walks in the Public Garden, our family had suddenly expanded to include Melanie and her two boys, McKey, age seven, and Robert, twelve. Of course, we would have had it no other way, but it meant planning meals, shopping for food, and cleaning house for five instead of two. I helped and so did Melanie as much as her health would allow, but Zoe assumed the bulk of caring for this new extended family.

Suddenly, it was as if we were parents again. Our space was no longer our own. The kitchen table became a desk on which to do homework. Melanie, who had been a teacher, patiently coped with her sons' resistance to do homework, but the atmosphere was tense with their resistance. Instead of a quiet cocktail as we prepared dinner, the kitchen pulsated with defiance. Then, when mealtime came, my Depression upbringing raged at food dumped in the garbage and milk poured into the sink because the boys had taken more then they could finish. I don't know if Zoe experienced this same annoyance, but she certainly must have sensed my suppressed anger. This was not how we had planned our near retirement years.

At Christmas time, the boys left for Virginia to be with their dad and stepmother. The three of us celebrated with a week long trip to Key West where we stayed in an old house with fans in the ceiling and chickens wandering on the street outside. Zoe didn't feel well before the trip, but hoped a change of scenery would help. Instead, pains in her stomach area become so intense that we had to catch an earlier flight home. A night or two later, the pains were unbearable and I rushed her to the emergency room at Salem Hospital. All night they prodded and probed while Zoe screamed in pain on the cold X-ray table. The resident night surgeon was reluctant to operate until he had some idea what was wrong. Finally, toward dawn she was taken into the operating room. Two hours later the doctor came out to tell me that they had done a resection on her intestine to remove a blockage. I went into the recovery room to find Zoe, white as the sheet that covered her, and so weak she couldn't talk.

When I came back later that day, she had been moved to a room. She was still weak and very pale. An IV was inserted directly into her neck in order to give her massive doses of antibiotics. It seemed that a quantity of toxins had escaped into her abdomen. Zoe spent several days in the hospital room which soon filled with flowers and cards from her many friends at work. Our little family visited daily.

Winter came and she was able to return to work, but it meant driving through slush and snow on crowded Salem streets until she reached the rush hour traffic on Rt. 128. When Digital surprised its employees by offering an early retirement option, Zoe jumped at it. For one thing, she could see the company was downsizing, but, I believe, the main reason was she was worn out. Zoe retired in May and for the first time in forty some years, she didn't have to get up and go to work in the morning.

Having a job, even when we were going to school, was always a part of our lives. At eighteen, soon after we were married in January 1951, Zoe got a part-time job at Marshall Field's in Chicago selling brassieres. We were students at the University of Chicago with a year and a half of college left, and we needed to work to make ends meet. I was twenty-one with a part-time job as a policy chaser at Lumberman's Mutual Insurance Company. When summer vacation came, we worked on a fire tower in Oregon, Zoe operating the radio and the firefinder while I managed a fire crew. Back at school, and nine months later, our son Danny was born just in time to interrupt Zoe's final exams. Still she graduated from college at age nineteen. We moved to Washington DC where I was an economic analyst for the CIA while Zoe took care of Danny. I left the CIA after a year to enlist in the Navy and eventually wound up in Japan where Zoe went back to work as a secretary for the Red Cross. After four years and four months in the Navy I entered an Episcopal Seminary in Evanston, Illinois, for three years of study to become a priest. Now we had three children, Danny, Melanie (born in Pensacola, Florida) and Martha (made in Japan but born at Great Lakes Naval Training Center). During the first year in Evanston, Zoe worked nights at a bank sorting checks. The next two years she taught in a nursery school where she was co-director. In addition to taking care of our kids, she attended National College of Education earning her Master's Degree the same time I graduated from Seminary. Zoe taught school for twenty years and then switched to Digital for another eleven years.

Retiring in the spring of 1992, she found herself at home everyday, confronting the management of our newly extended family. There were good times: redecorating the old house on Gregory Street, cooking dinners on our back deck and taking occasional trips. But given all the things that were happening in our family and with Zoe's health, she was having a tougher time adjusting to retirement than I realized.

When Zoe was ten, her cousin had given her his cocker spaniel, Patsy, because he was leaving for the Navy. Patsy went with Zoe as her family moved from Chicago to Easthampton, Massachusetts, and then New York City. She was Zoe's close companion during a time when Zoe was having to make new friends in unfamiliar surroundings. Perhaps it was the memory of Patsy that led Zoe to make the trip to the Boston Animal Rescue League. Some years later she told me that the reason Bear meant so much to her was because his love for her was unconditional. Like Patsy before him, he loved her just as she was. And that's how he loved her for the rest of his life.

Two years later, in March of 1994, I turned 65, but the idea of retirement didn't seem possible financially. Not that I wasn't getting tired of the politics at work. One day as I was driving to work, I passed two men my age who were ambling down the sidewalk for a morning walk to the beach. How I would love to be able to do that, I thought. Imagine, getting up early not because I had to go to work, but because I wanted to go for a walk to the beach with a good friend. That picture weighed on my mind until one day I asked Zoe if she thought it might be possible for me to retire as soon as I completed ten years with the Massachusetts Port Authority the end of July. We started looking at the cash flow from Social Security and my pension as well as the income from the lump sum retirement Zoe had invested from Digital. Much to our surprise, it looked possible. So on July 30, 1994, I retired. The first thing we did was buy a Ford pickup with extended cab and a used fifth-wheel camping trailer.

A few days after retiring from Massport, Zoe, Bear and I were on our way to Cape Hatteras. With our little trailer hooked on behind our pickup, it looked like the doors of freedom had opened for us. We could go where we wanted, when we wanted. Bear gave us his dead pan look as he sat in the seat between us, but I knew he was happy.

Chapter Three

If You Could?

*I*t isn't often you can point to a particular moment when your life turned dramatically in a totally different direction. I thought the future was set. In 1997 we had moved from Gregory Street into a one story house where, as old age began to take its toll, we wouldn't have to climb stairs. In the basement off our garage was a bedroom and bath for McKey when he came to visit us from his father's home in Virginia. The backyard had a fence so Bear and Melanie's newly acquired dog, Clara, could roam at their leisure. The yard was small and easily mowed by our new lawn mower with large rear wheels. And we lived two houses away from the Waterside Cemetery, thus facilitating the last trip of our lives.

We had been in Marblehead for seven years. The publishing of my first novel and the subsequent whirlwind of speaking engagements and book signings had been a heady experience. My second novel was published to much lesser acclaim, but I kept writing. As I struggled with a third novel, I found myself bumping into blocks at every turn.

What I didn't know, or allow myself to realize, was how unhappy Zoe was living in Marblehead. She wasn't interested in sailboats, which I was content to watch from the security of Lighthouse Point as they swept majestically into the ocean. To find some purpose in our narrowing existence, she read to a blind woman in one of Marblehead's convalescent homes. Bear went with her and put his head into the woman's lap so she could dig her fingers into his fur and rub his ears as Zoe read. But as I said, Marblehead is a sailor's town and if you don't sail, you're an observer, a non-participant in life's flow.

Even Bear was unhappy. He and Clara were cramped into the narrow confines of our fenced back yard, and able to venture forth only on the end of a six foot leash. And there were only so many walks we could do in a day.

One summer evening in 1999 as Zoe and I were having cocktails while a steak sizzled on the charcoal grill, I asked her help on a sticky point with which I was struggling in my novel. In the story a fifty-five year old woman wanted to leave her high-powered executive position for something that would give her a connection to life's simpler values. I explained this background to Zoe and then asked, "What would you think if I have her give up her career in business and move to a small rural town to bake bread?"

"Bake bread?" she grunted with disgust.

"That's the most boring thing I can imagine."

"Oh!" I was taken aback at her vehemence. "Okay then. If you could do anything you wanted, what would you do?"

Without even a pause, she said, "I'd raise Newfoundlands."

"You mean, breed them?"

"Yes. Bear's half Newfoundland, and the best dog in all the world. So just imagine what a full blooded Newfoundland would be. And then imagine a bunch of them."

"In this house?"

"Of course not. I'd live in a place that has a pond so they can swim. I'd still want a small house, big enough for you and me and Mel and her boys when they visit, but all on one floor. I don't want to spend a lot of time house cleaning."

"While you're imagining, where would you live?"

"I think," and she paused for a moment, "I think somewhere near Easthampton, out in western Massachusetts. I loved it there when I was ten."

I took a sip of scotch, then said, "You're not kidding, are you."

"No." She leaned back in her deck chair and gazed wistfully at the flowering plum trees in the back yard. "I don't really like it here. I'm only sixty-six and I'm not ready to settle down to a rocking chair."

"You scare me when you talk like this. I'm seventy. I thought moving here was the last move of our lives."

She didn't answer. She'd said all she wanted to say.

In the forty-nine years we'd been married, we'd hardly ever labored over decisions. When buying a house, for instance, and we've bought many over the years, we had only to look at each other, then say, "Yes, this is the one." I guess, unconsciously, we have a common vision of the house we want, and when we find it, we buy it. Now, as the possibility of an entirely new career exploded into our lives like a thunderbolt, we had only to see the excitement in each other's eyes to know that it was the thing to do.

I removed the steaks from the grill and wrapped them in foil, while Zoe turned on the computer. We got a map of Massachusetts and discovered that Easthampton is in Hampshire county. Zoe asked the computer for a listing of real estate agents in that county and up came the name of Jim Molyneux. Realizing that part of our impetuousness might have been due to the scotch, we decided to eat our steaks and wait until morning to call the agent.

When morning came, we walked onto our back deck with our cups of coffee, and contemplated the tiny yard. In Bear's eyes we saw, or wanted to see, a longing for wide open spaces and a pond in which he could swim.

"Let's do it," I said.

"Of course," Zoe replied, as if she'd been waiting for me to get on board her dream.

When I think about it, my willingness to strike off into uncharted territory is something I probably inherited from my mom. In 1900, when she was eight, her father was killed in a train accident, leaving her mother and four sisters without any means of support. They moved from Tennessee to Colorado where the five daughters worked on the vegetable farm of a friend. Soon they built a cabin and homesteaded on the western slope of the Rockies. From there they opened a millinery shop in Hotchkiss and later a boardinghouse in Colorado Springs. They were strong, competent women four of whom lived to more than 98 years old, one even reaching 101.

We called Jim Molyneux who told us he had three houses he thought might fit our needs. The next day Zoe, Melanie and I, plus Bear and Clara, made the three hour trip to his office in South Worthington. The first house was located on the Deerfield River which would provide an excellent swimming pool for Newfoundlands, but the house was a wreck. The second house was small and all on one floor. Actually it was a bit too small, but an adjacent barn held the possibilities for expansion. The water, which the property claimed, was a tiny stream hidden in cattails that had already dried up in the summer's heat.

"I think you might like this next house," Jim said as we rounded a bend and crossed an old bridge, "but it's rather large." There, behind a rail fence, was a huge, two story, brown house with attached carriage barn. A small sign on the house said, "c. 1812". To the left of the house was an apple orchard and to the right, a large lawn and flower garden. "The owners are both at work," Jim said, "so I can't take you inside but we can look around the grounds."

With Bear and Clara on leashes, we peered in windows at the wide pine planks that made up the floors and at fireplaces in the family room and living room. "The whole back of the property is the Westfield River," Jim said. "There's a path down to the river at the end of the garden."

Bear was ready to go, as if he already knew the way. Stone steps beneath shading maple trees led down to the river. We unhooked the dogs and down they went, across a bit of sand and into a pool of crystal clear water off the main course of the rushing river. Half floating, half standing on the sandy bottom, Bear looked back at us with what had to be a smile. He'd made up his mind.

The next day we returned to the house. After the long drive on crowded highways, we turned off Highway 9 onto "old 9" where the road used to go, and it was like entering the peace and quiet of Shangri-la.

"How far do you have to go to shop?" I asked Jim.

"Oh, not far. 'Bout twenty miles."

We met the owners, and toured the house. On the west side was an apartment with two bedrooms, a kitchenette and living room. The main house had a large living room cooled by a gentle breeze coming through windows on both the front and the back of the house. On the east side of the central entrance, was a family room and dining area just off a modernized kitchen, the only up-to-date room in the house. A door led to a large mud room from which another door opened into the carriage barn. Upstairs was a bathroom, very large bedroom with an adjoining room that could be a study, another small bedroom and large room that could be a workroom. Zoe and I eyed the room with the study, and Melanie the other bedroom and workroom. The boys could use the west wing apartment when they were at home.

After touring the house, the three of us walked back down to the river to give the dogs one last chance to swim. Across the river were woods climbing the slopes of the valley walls as far as we could see. We each waited for someone else to speak. The house, after all, was anything but small and it was two stories. I was thinking the maintenance on a two hundred year old house would be considerable. Then I saw that look in Zoe's eyes and together we said, "Let's buy it."

"Oh thank God," Melanie said. "I was so afraid you wouldn't want it because it's so big."

Bear, standing belly deep in the pool and hearing our shouts of joy, barked his approval.

Two days later, after looking at comparative house prices in the area, we made an offer on the house which was accepted by the owners. We put our Marblehead house on the market and began the process of arranging financing. The second week of October 1999, we moved in.

How strange it was that moving to this house was like coming home. There was the rural quality that I remember about visits to the farm north of my hometown, Flint, Michigan, where my father grew up. The miles and miles of forests reminded me of the many days I spent as a teenager hiking and camping in the woods. For Zoe it must have brought back thoughts of Easthampton where she lived when she was ten. And for me, I soon learned that we had moved only thirty minutes away from Hadley, where the first Montague family lived in 1660, from which a later Montague, Daniel Nathaniel, moved in 1837 to the farm where my dad grew up.

After living in several different states and even abroad in Japan, we had come home.

Chapter Four

Second Birth

We have moved the whelping box from the study to the end of our bed, where, hopefully, Bess and her six puppies will have a better chance of enduring the heat. The weather is unbearably hot with 90 degrees during the day and over 80 at night. The study was too confining. Even in our bedroom we have a problem. Bess's puppies, which now weigh about five pounds and are two weeks old, are still too young to have a fan blowing on them. Bess, on the other hand, is so hot she hates to leave the direct path of one of our fans. Two nights ago the temperature reached 85 and Zoe had to take each of the pups to the bathroom and cool them off with a dip in the sink.

Bess solved her own problem as far as feeding the puppies is concerned. She jumps onto the bed and waits for us to bring her puppies to her. We line them up and each finds a place to nurse. There's more air circulating around the bed so Bess is not so uncomfortable, and the puppies are happy to crawl around on the soft bed. And they do crawl. Before we know it, Miss Red has slipped between Bess's back legs and is heading for the right side of the bed. No sooner do we return her to the feeding station, then Mr. Orange is doing his breast stroke across the blanket for the other side of the bed. Eventually the puppies finish nursing and fall asleep. If it's nighttime and I'm alone, I quickly scoop them up, one in each hand, and return them to the whelping box.

Standing watches with the puppies at night can get old in a hurry, but we can't take the chance of having Bess lie or step on one of her little ones. When I'm in the bedroom lying in bed with one eye on a book and the other on the puppies, Zoe is in Melanie's workroom asleep on the futon. At midnight when she comes to the bedroom, I go to the workroom. We've been doing this for two weeks and we still have at least a week to go. I feel like I'm in jet lag without the pleasure of having been to Europe. Also, I miss Zoe.

It's now three in the morning, and the puppies are beginning to whine and cry. They last ate at midnight, so it's time for Bess to feed them again. Bess is asleep in the hall where a fan is blowing full blast from the bathroom window, through the door and down the hall.

"Come on Bess," I say, shaking her shoulder, "time to feed your puppies." She doesn't move. What she's waiting for is the snack we usually give her before she feeds her puppies. I open a can of dog food and pass it by her nose. She's up in a second and following me and the can of food into the bedroom. As she passes the whelping box the puppies catch her scent and immediately wake up. They turn up their sirens, and head off in six different directions in search of Mom. While Bess is gobbling her snack, I watch the puppies swim across the blanket in the whelping box. Over in the corner, my eye falls on Miss Red.

"What have we here?" I say to Bess. She ignores me as her big tongue pushes her food bowl against the leg of the dresser. "Miss Red is trying to stand."

While the other puppies are using their front feet like flippers to pull themselves around the box, Miss Red is making a feeble attempt to get her front feet under her and stand up. She looks like a middle-aged guy doing more pushups than he can handle. As she pushes herself up, her head shakes, her shoulders vibrate from the strain, and she collapses. Undaunted, she tries again to stand.

"Go for it, Miss Red," I say. And she does. She gets her front up and drags her backend in the direction of Mom who's about to get into the box and clean up her puppies.

In another part of the box, Mr. White is up on all fours ready to give walking a try. As one of his back legs takes a step, his front legs buckle and down he goes. This walking is complicated business.

I'm reminded of a series of pictures I once saw of the evolution of the mammal as it crawled out of the primordial ooze onto dry land. As it moved through thousands of years of evolution, the pictorial frames showed it pulling itself along on flippers like a seal climbing onto a rock. Then its flippers evolved into feet and legs which lifted it off the ground until it was standing on all fours. This is what I'm witnessing tonight, a kind of ontogeny recapitulating phylogeny.

Bess finishes her snack and steps over the edge of the whelping box to lap up the bits of puppy poop I've missed and to clean her puppies' backends. This is not what the puppies want. They want to find those nipples that are exuding that delicious aroma of mother's milk. But Bess persists. Her enormous tongue flips them onto their backs and licks their butts so vigorously they are tossed around and pushed across the box. When the ablutions are completed, she jumps onto the bed and gets ready for me to bring them to her. Picking up Miss Purple, I notice another first. Her eyes are open just a slit and she seems to be looking at me. I check the other pups as I pick them up. Miss Green's eyes are beginning to open, too. And her fur is showing signs of curls behind her neck.

All of a sudden they have changed from squirming, seal-like creatures to baby dogs determined to get up on all fours and have a look at the world. Later I learn that breeders call this the second birth.

In 1952 we had another summer that was hot as hell. We were living in Shirley Duke Apartments in Alexandria, Virginia. Danny was two months old, having been born just when Zoe was scheduled to take her final exams in May at the University of Chicago. This meant she would have to take them *in absentia* in the fall. She was holding Danny with one hand as he nursed, and had a text book in the other. The two-bedroom apartment had no cross-ventilation and, of course, no air conditioning. Zoe was nineteen and I was twenty-three. What did we know about taking care of a baby? The poor kid had heat rash and colic. In the evening when I came home from work, we would sit on our front stoop hoping for a breeze. During the day Zoe was stuck in this oven of an apartment because we had no car. I was off at my first real job as an economic analyst for the Central Intelligence Agency. I worked in a World War Two temporary building, which was also without air conditioning, near the Lincoln Memorial.

Zoe felt trapped in the apartment, and I felt threatened by Senator Joseph McCarthy who considered anyone from that pinko University of Chicago to be a communist sympathizer.

At night, when I wanted to knit up the raveled sleeve of care, I had to take turns with Zoe walking Danny around our hot apartment hoping he'd go to sleep. The poor little guy just screamed and screamed.

And then one day something wonderful happened. I came home from work and Zoe said, "Watch."

She lifted Danny up in the air and kissed his bare tummy. Danny smiled, and for once it wasn't a gas pain. She did it again and he giggled. "Here," she said, "you do it."

I lifted him up and planted a slobbery kiss on his belly button. He giggled. For the first time, he was more than just a diaper-messing, spitting-up, non-sleeping screamer. He was a human being. He was interacting with us. And with his giggles and smiles he helped us to help him bear the heat of that awful summer. It was his second birth.

In 1954 Melanie was five months old when Zoe brought her and Danny to Japan where I, having left CIA, was serving a tour of duty with the Navy. We lived in a tiny house as one of three American families in a town of 50,000

Japanese. I missed most of Melanie's transformation from infant to a charming baby because I had left for Japan three months after she was born, but no sooner did she arrive than her winning personality took me and our Japanese neighbors by storm. Her big round eyes and blond hair caused all the mama-sans to stop on the street and declare, "*Ah so deska.*"

When I think of our third child, Martha, as a baby, I see her at age six months in 1956, sitting in the bathroom sink of the first house we owned in Glen Ellyn, Illinois. Enclosed in her sleeping bag, she had somehow climbed into the sink from the toilet and was squeezing toothpaste from a tube into her mouth. She looked at me with an uncertain smile that said, "Am I doing something wrong?" I called Zoe who brought the camera and we took her picture. Now it hangs in our bathroom, and we can't pass it by without smiling.

The puppies are falling asleep and drifting off Bess's nursing stations, all except adventurous Mr. Blue who is pulling himself toward the edge of the bed to see if he can fly to the floor. I snatch him up first and put him in the box, then I pick up the other sleepyheads, one in each hand and return them to the box.

When all the pups are back and Bess has departed for the somewhat cooler hall, the crying starts again. They still think they're hungry. With each pant of air, they attach a cry. "Waa," pant, "waa," pant, "waa," pant, all in rapid succession. Wandering around the box, they wonder where the chuck wagon's gone. Three of them have formed a puppy clot, wrapping themselves up together in a ball. Mr. Orange is up on all fours. He takes a step, his front leg gives way and he tumbles over on his back. Four legs flail the air until he manages to roll over again onto his tummy. Then he falls asleep. Soon the room is quiet.

At four-thirty the sky above Deer Hill takes on a blue-gray hue that silhouettes the jagged tops of pine trees. I wait until five and then wake up Zoe with the news of the puppies starting to stand.

"Really," she says. "I've got to see this."

We sit on the end of our bed and watch the puppies in the whelping box. They begin to wake up and cry. Just for Zoe, Miss Red performs her now famous act of lifting herself up on her front legs. As her whole body shakes with the effort, she gets her back legs under her and rises up on all fours. We applaud. She takes a bow, and collapses.

Zoe picks her up and kisses her nose.

"Look at her head," she says. "Isn't she beautiful?" Newfoundland wrinkles are forming on her muzzle. Her head is broad. Her ears are little flaps. The fur on her back is beginning to curl. Zoe stares into her eyes, and Miss Red opens one and stares back blankly.

"Did you see that?" Zoe says.

"Yes," I say, and I share Zoe's joy. But mostly I'm thinking how nice it is just to be sitting here on the bed beside Zoe. I'll be glad when these three weeks of constant watching are over.

Chapter Five

Storm

*I*t's the second week of August, 2004, our fifth year in this old house we've come to love. It's five-thirty in the morning and still the sun hasn't risen over the hills surrounding our valley. How soon the darkness lingers and the light retreats as the earth turns from its summer solstice. The grueling period of constantly watching the puppies is over, and they are now five and a half weeks old. They have graduated from the whelping box to an exercise pen, which is a series of fence sections that can be shaped into a circle. Breeders call it an X-pen. As I come down to the dining area off the kitchen and family room, I attempt to sneak by the puppies in their X-pen. I walk quietly so as not to wake our little friends, hoping I can make the coffee and return to bed before Zoe and I have to feed them and the grown-up dogs.

In the dim light of the dining room I see six loaves of black puppy fur. One step toward the kitchen, two, and a head pops up. Then another and another. Soon six heads with twelve black, shiny eyes are following me into the kitchen. One lets go with a raspy bark. Another cries. Now they're all awake and crowding the side of the pen next to the kitchen. I bid them good morning and make the coffee, then return to the family room with James Joyce's *Portrait of the Artist as a Young Man*, and settle down to wait for the coffee. I'm still in view of the puppies. They watch me. Finally they lie down and go back to sleep. I take a cup of coffee up to Zoe who is still in bed. So our day begins.

At six o'clock Ellie jumps onto our bed. She is huge and towers over us as we lie against our pillows reading. Looking down at us lovingly like Thurber's dog watching a bug, she tells us that according to her contract we feed her breakfast at six. Zoe negotiates a few more minutes by rubbing her chest. A twelve-inch drool forms on her slack lips letting us know we don't have much more time. "All right," Zoe says, and Ellie leaps from the bed with a loud bark rallying the other four Newfoundlands in a charge down the stairs. One of the first alterations we made in the house was to put a second handrail on the stairs should we find ourselves in the forefront of this charge of the heavy black brigade.

Lights come on in the kitchen, dining area and dog room (the former mud room). As Zoe prepares the dogs' breakfast, I look at the floor of the X-pen. The blanket and towels are yellow with damp pee and smeared with brown puppy poop. As I squeeze into the pen, two puppies escape through the opening. Frantically, I try to shove them back in as three more escape. I feel like the Dutch boy sticking his finger into the leaking dike, but unable to stanch the flow. "Oh, the hell with it," I say and let them all out into the family room. They're delighted and head for the dining room table, which is now sitting in the family room, to poop among the chair legs. I remove the sodden towels and throw a couple of dry ones down to cover the damp blanket while we wait for Bess to finish eating. When she's done she leads her brood back into the pen where they glom onto her teats while she's still standing. They look like a picture I remember from my high school Latin book of Romulus and Remus, kneeling on the ground with mouths raised and lips latched onto the teats of a wolf. The sound of sucking is deafening. Bess can only take so much of this puppy feeding and is soon ready to leave. I have felt the sharp teeth of these little Newfies and I can understand why she wants to leave.

Trading places with Bess I remain in the pen while Zoe passes me three large platters of specially prepared puppy food: dried puppy pellets which she mushed and soaked overnight, yogurt, a can of puppy food and evaporated milk. I put them down and step aside as the puppies look this way and that, sensing that something good is happening. One spots the food and runs to it, landing in the platter with his two front paws. Soon they are all gathering around the platters and focusing on food. In less than two minutes, the platters are clean.

Later that morning, I'm sitting by the outdoor pen attached to the shed behind the west wing. The puppies stand on sturdy legs that sometimes give way as they run across the pea stones and blanket that cover the floor of the pen. Their heads are broad, their furry ears floppy, their muzzles wrinkled and their chests broad. Dark brown eyes stare with an intensity that draws me into their souls. I smile, then laugh at their antics. My spirits are lifted.

Bess asks me to open the door to the pen. It's not from any maternal desire to feed them. It's because there are some unfinished crumbs from tiny dog biscuits lying on the blanket. She enters and wanders about scooping up fragments, when suddenly the puppies realize Mom has joined them. Immediately they come running and tumbling over each other, pursuing her as she ambles about the pen. They catch her and line up under her belly slurping vigorously. As Bess walks, they tumble off, then scurry after her for one last drink before she asks to be let out.

Two of the puppies have already made

trips to the vet. Soon after they were born, Mr. White's tail was apparently stepped on by Bess. Her claw cut all the way through his tail bone near the tip. The vet said it had to be taken off and cauterized to prevent infection. In that instant when Bess's paw cut the tail, White lost his status as a possible show dog. A few days later we noticed that Miss Purple's tail wagged only to the right. Afraid that a growth was limiting the tail movement, she too went to the vet. There was no growth, but at the point where the coccyx attaches to the tail, the bone was dislocated, possibly from another misstep by Bess. Even if Purple and White can't compete as show dogs, they will make good pets. And, if their hips and hearts are okay, there is no reason why they can't produce good puppies since their lineage is excellent. There are also other opportunities to demonstrate the qualities of the Newfoundland. They can be water rescue dogs, therapy dogs, or they can learn carting and tracking, and can compete for obedience and agility. That's all well and good, but as I watch Miss Purple wag her tail only to the right, and Mr. White vibrate his half-tail, I beg their forgiveness for not having watched them more carefully when they were still in the whelping box.

Late afternoon and a thunder storm is coming. I can hear its distant rumblings and see the sky darkening. Salmon steaks are roasting on the grill, and smoke from the hickory chips I've added to the charcoal is clouding out the vent with an aromatic promise of good food to come. I sit by the fence inside the dog yard, a glass of scotch resting on the rail of the fence. The gate to the outdoor pen is open and the puppies are exploring the dog yard. Mr. Blue has found a dried leaf and carries it triumphantly, head held high, toward Miss Red, until he forgets why he wanted to show it to her and lies down. Miss Green is chewing on a piece of grass that has poked its head through the fence. Mr. Orange, the largest of the puppies, is chewing on Mr. White's back leg, while he is having a teeth baring, open mouth battle with Miss Purple. To think that these fifteen pound puppies were less than a pound and half only five and a half weeks ago! I watch them amazed as their nascent nerves organize and coordinate their strengthening muscles. How quickly they have graduated from sleeping and eating to exploring with an inquisitive eye the wonders of the world around them.

The thunder rolls and Zoe comes out to the yard. "Better get them into the pen," she says. The pen is an eight by twelve foot enclosure beneath a metal roof. Zoe carries Mr. Orange to the pen and goes in, shutting the gate behind her. I hand the other puppies to her over the top of the fence. We used to carry them two at a time, but now they're too heavy. When they're all in, I call "Puppy, puppy!" over the fence at the rear of pen, and Zoe skips out the gate at the front. They don't understand why their dog yard fun has been cut short. They cluster by the fence complaining with cries and abortive barks.

I return to my chair on the other side of the yard. I'll wait for the first drops of rain before I roll the charcoal grill under the shed roof behind the barn. From my chair by the fence I look down through a jungle of leaves and branches to the river. It flashes with excitement at the prospects of replenishment from the coming rain. The wind picks up and bends the tops of the hundred foot high spruce beyond our orchard sending crested waxwings helter-skelter into the air. Puffs of ill formed clouds hurry overhead to make way for the dark gray, massive thunderheads muscling in from the west. Then all falls quiet, like the hush in a theater as the house lights dim and the curtain quivers in preparation for raising.

I sip my scotch and watch a tiny bug no

larger than a period flying on wings so small that their flutter blurs the shape of its minuscule body. Does it have any idea where its urgent beating of wings will take it? How does it even have room in that microscopic head for a brain to instruct its flight? Yet, somewhere in that weightless gauze of a body is the same quality of life that invigorates and vitalizes the puppies. It's the same life quality that oozes out of the mud down by the river and produces a thousand species of green plants. I turn in my chair and look back at Deer Hill to the east and see the bowers of foliage laid one upon the other like light and dark green pillows piled at the head of a giant bedstead. The quantity and profundity of all these vessels of life's essence fills me with awe.

The little bug flutters across the hushed stage before me. It speaks. "For your evening's entertainment, sun's fire and earth's vapors are pleased to bring you a sound and light show." I applaud. The bug bows and floats off. Without further delay, the curtain rises to a flash of lightening and a crack of thunder.

I run between globular rain drops to pull the grill under the metal shed roof. A sudden wind catches my plastic chair and blows it over. Rain out-thunders the thunder as it hammers on the metal roof. My scotch, still sitting on the rail, is filling with water. Oh well.

I look across the dog yard at the puppies' pen. They are asleep, rolled into a large black ball. I would like to wake them, huddle down with them, and together watch and listen to the zinging flashes and the explosive clash of ionized air. This is no small show. The stage is miles wide and thousands of feet high. The actors are as ancient as time itself. Their message undeniable. The plot is about what is. In all the world there is no other place or time where I would rather be than here beneath this metal roof, deafened by the drumming rain.

As suddenly as it began, it stops. The curtain falls with the last few drops of rain. I step out into the dog yard. Leaves still heavy with water, bend like pitchers emptying their contents. The river laughs, climbing its banks and leaping rocks. A crested waxwing lands on the very tip of one of the towering spruce. The pea stones in the dog yard glisten. A puppy raises his head and looks at me, then lowers it. My glass of scotch, filled with rain, runneth over.

I carry the roasted salmon, golden brown, into the house.

Chapter Six

Jamie

*T*he difference between a job and retirement is I don't have a boss. Everything else is pretty much the same. First off, there's a full load of work to do everyday, and second, I still have to get along with the people around me. Add to this five dogs and, right now, six puppies. But the big thing is, I don't have a boss with his or her agenda that might not agree with mine. Along with the other people and the dogs, I'm on my own, doing what needs to be done.

This morning it's raining — I might say cascading — as the remnants of Hurricane Charlie move through New England. At five-thirty the puppies are calling for breakfast. We kick Ellie and Patsy off our bed where they have been pressing Zoe and me together as if in a vise, and go downstairs. I come into the family room where we have the puppies in the X-pen. Immediately they see me. "Yip, Yip! He's coming! He's coming! Yip, Yip!" I put on my rain coat, quickly open the screen door off the dining room and then the door to the X-pen which is only three feet away. Like logs in a river, they jumble up and tumble toward the door, then stop and bunch up at the step down to the outside. I push. Some fall, some jump and soon they are all outside in the pouring rain. Dancing into the dog yard I start my morning song. "Poops and pees, poops and pees. Let's all have some poops and pees." They gather around my legs under my raincoat. We've been outside for thirty seconds and already they're matted with rain. Carefully I move one foot into a space where there are no puppies, then another. They follow. Then Miss Red takes off across the yard on an urgent mission to answer nature's call, and poops on a section of hose. Mr. Orange follows. About this time Patsy comes out to the yard for the same purpose I have the puppies there. Immediately, the puppies rush over to Patsy. "Are you Mommy?" they ask huddling under her looking for teats.

"No! No!" Patsy answers. "Get out from under me. I'm busy." When they don't move, she runs to another part of the yard. The puppies are hot on her trail. She tries to squat, but Mr. White is in the way. Again she takes off. Like Keystone Kops after a bank robber, the puppies, fumbling and bumping into each other, pursue her. Again she cocks her tail and lowers her backend. Too late for Mr. Blue. He gets one right on the top of his head. Fortunately it's solid and it rolls off. Patsy returns to the house for her breakfast and the puppies resume wandering the dog yard, oblivious of the rain, pooping and peeing.

When Zoe has fed the big dogs, Bess comes out to the yard. "Oh joy! Oh rapture!" sing the puppies. "There's Mommy for sure." And they gather under the shelter of her big body for the first snack of the morning. As they nurse, I spread a dry, fresh blanket in the outdoor pen under the metal roof. Zoe is in the kitchen preparing their three platters of food.

Let me say that Bess is really cool. She and I have figured out how to maneuver the puppies where we want them, when we want them. I leave the shelter of the shed and go over to Bess. "Okay sweetheart. Let's put 'em in the outdoor pen." Without another word from me, Bess heads for the pen, the puppies chasing after her. Inside, out of the rain, she lets them nurse for another minute or two, then walks to the back of the pen while I stand by the gate. "Now!" I say, and she shakes them loose and dashes out while I go inside and close the gate behind me. Zoe's head appears in the dining room door and she calls something which I can't hear because of the rain drumming on the metal roof, but I assume she's asking if we're ready. I wave for her to bring the platters. She does, and hands them to me over the fence. I place them on the ground with two puppies to a platter. Another day is underway.

There'll be no mowing of the lawn again today, which is unfortunate. We've had more than a week of rainy days and the grass is getting so long I'll need a harvester. But there are other jobs to do. On the refrigerator is a list: trim dead branches from trees, paint around window inserts (thirty-one new thermopane windows were installed last month), repair storm windows, remove rust from Subaru (eleven years old), get fireplace ready for the new pellet stove (coming in two days), Clorox the dog yard (twice weekly), etc. Zoe has her lists too: medicine and pills for the dogs, correspondence with other dog breeders, washing and grooming the dogs, training each dog, endless washing and drying of towels and blankets used for the puppies, to say nothing of shopping for food, cooking and taking care of family finances and bill paying (thank God she takes care of it). And everyday we clean and vacuum, especially now that Mattie, our year old puppy, is shedding quantities of coat throughout the house.

Today is shopping day, not because we shop on a certain day, but because we've run out of food. The dogs follow Zoe to the door to say good bye. "I'll be back in a little while," she says and slips out the door. All the dogs but

Jamie run to the play yard where they can watch Zoe drive away in our Astro van. Jamie remains by the door where she will sit, looking up at it, until Zoe returns.

Jamie is Zoe's dog, or rather, Zoe is Jamie's human. From the day we brought Jamie home, she has remained attached to Zoe. She sleeps on the floor on Zoe's side of the bed, she sits in the middle of the kitchen while Zoe cooks and beside Zoe at the computer, occasionally nudging her arm. When Zoe goes upstairs, Jamie plods along behind her. When she showers, Jamie lies in the hall outside the closed door. For five years, since we brought Jamie into our home, she's been Zoe's shadow.

The fall of 1999, when we decided to raise Newfoundlands and buy a house in West Cummington, we embarked on the task of obtaining our first Newfoundland. Our initial sortie into the world of these gentle giants was to attend a dog show in New Hampshire. Unfortunately we were a day late, but a Newfoundland owner who had not yet departed told us we should get in touch with Jane Thibault in Connecticut. Zoe called Jane and asked if we could come to a water training day held at her kennel, Nashua-auke, the following Sunday. When we arrived many cars and

Newfoundlands were already there. Along the bank of a large pond located on her property were several people participating in training exercises with their dogs. One dog was carrying a rescue line to a person waving her arms far out in the water. Another dog was swimming out to a "stranded" boat and, taking its painter in its mouth, began towing it to shore. Yet another dog leaped from the back of a boat and swam to a person supposedly drowning, then pulled him to shore.

Jane had at least thirty Newfoundlands in runs and cages as well as lying on sofas in her living room watching TV. She is a loving person both to her animals and her friends, the kind of person you want to hug, which I now do whenever I see her. How she manages to feed and care for so many animals is beyond me. Even while her friends were training their dogs by the pond, she was scooting around her property on a golf cart, feeding her dogs.

We met many owners that day, each of whom had some advice about finding a dog and what was needed to provide for a Newfoundland. Jane suggested that Zoe get in touch with Betty McDonnell in New Jersey to see if she might have a female. (The reader might as well know that I have trouble with the word "bitch". It's not only acceptable for a female dog, it's correct. But that isn't the way I grew up with the word. Henceforth, I shall refer to female Newfoundlands as dogs, girls or, in the case of our five Newfoundlands, the ladies. Back to Jane speaking to Zoe about Betty.) "She'll want to know that you're capable of caring for a Newfoundland," Jane advised, "so be prepared."

We hadn't yet moved into our new house, but we made a trip to West Cummington and took pictures of the house, the grounds and the river where the dogs would be able to swim. Zoe sent these pictures to Betty along with a letter explaining our previous experience with dogs. Betty said she'd be attending a water trials test in Connecticut and asked Zoe to meet her there. When we got there, Betty was going a mile-a-minute entering her dogs in the trials, but we found some time to talk. Apparently she found us acceptable as potential Newfoundland owners because she offered Zoe an opportunity to co-own with her a three year old bitch (Betty speaking) who already had her championship. The dog's name was Jamielee.

We picked up Jamie from Betty's kennel the middle of October, 1999. While Jamie knew her way around a show ring, she hadn't had much chance for social development. We wondered what would happen when we brought her home and into the new house that Bear and

Clara had claimed as their territory two weeks earlier. Bear and Clara got along okay. Clara accepted that he was the boss, having joined our family when she was a puppy. For Jamie's entry into the house, we put the other two dogs in the west wing. Jamie entered and, aware of the scent of the other dogs, began a thorough tour of the house. She was moving so fast we couldn't keep up with her. Eventually we found her in the upstairs bathroom sitting in the bathtub seeming quite content.

With Jamie on a secure leash, we introduced Bear, also on a leash. We kept the dogs on opposite sides of the room. There was no growling but much guarded reconnoitering. Slowly we reduced the distance between them as they seemed to accept each other's presence. Bear was always a sucker for a female even though there was nothing he could do if he wanted to. Jamie even did a little girlish dance. After a while it appeared that they would get along. A year later, however, a contest for dominance developed one day over a bone in the narrow confines of the kitchen. There was one hell of a fight with teeth locked in jowls and on ears. Zoe, Melanie and I tried unsuccessfully to pull them apart. When Zoe got too close, one of the dog's teeth got hold of her finger, almost taking the end off. Her screams so scared the two dogs that they separated, but she was on the verge of going into shock. We called 911 and in a matter of minutes were engulfed by Cummington emergency squads. We had an ambulance, police car, dog officer's car and the cars of five volunteer EMTs parked in front of our house. In the living room were eleven people from our new community whom we hadn't even met yet. Zoe was on the sofa being administered to by EMTs, the chief of police was asking how it had happened and the dog officer was checking on the dogs' rabies vaccinations. They decided Zoe should be taken to Cooley Dickinson Hospital in Northampton, but before she would leave, she asked to see the two dogs. We brought Bear in first. He was very concerned about Zoe's condition. Separately, Jamie was brought into the living room. Head down, with big sorrowful eyes looking up at Zoe, Jamie apologized. Then Zoe was whisked off to the emergency room. The finger was saved.

After this fight, old Bear yielded to Jamie's dominance and simply withdrew from the chain of command. Clara was another story. At any moment Clara's Manchester Terrier genes might assert themselves and she would nip at Jamie. Jamie considered these attacks a challenge to her dominance and she'd fight back, catching

Clara in her jaws. The blood would flow and off we'd go to the vet with Clara.

Clara, who could be so lovable, was also a hunter. Her heritage flashed to the surface when least wanted. When we still lived in Marblehead a few years before, we'd visit Zoe's college roommate, Pat Brown, in Maine each summer. We had often taken Bear who would lie serenely on the porch during morning coffee or evening cocktails and watch the gulls and osprey circle over lobster pots out in the bay. On this visit we had planned to take Clara also. With the fifth-wheel trailer in tow behind our pickup, Zoe and I and the two dogs went to Maine, first spending a couple of days camping in the trailer. On the day we were to go to Pat's we were walking the two dogs off leash. They had fallen behind us some distance when we heard wild barking. Running back, we saw Clara with an animal in her mouth shaking it vigorously in an effort to break its neck. When we got up to her, we saw it was a skunk which was in the process of liberally spraying both Clara and Bear. The smell of musk finally got to Clara and she dropped the skunk, but not before both dogs were anointed with one of the vilest odors in the universe. We tied both dogs to a tree some distance from the trailer while we sought advise from local people about how to deal with the smell. Tomato juice was the solution of choice and I set off for the grocery store. When I walked into the small country store, people drew back. Some distance away a clerk called to me. "I think you want tomato juice. It's over there. Leave the money on the counter."

Needless to say, we didn't go to Pat's cottage. Not wanting to pollute the trailer, we put the dogs in the pickup's jump seat and drove straight home with the windows open. As far as I'm concerned, tomato juice is an old wives' tale. It doesn't work, nor do all the other remedies they sell in the pet stores. If your dog gets skunked, you live with it until it goes away. Sandalwood incense helps in the house, somewhat.

I think it was the second night after we'd moved into the new house that Clara's second encounter with living in the wilds occurred. We didn't have a fence as yet so we had to escort the dogs out the back door when they wanted to pee before bedtime. The previous owner had put up spotlights in the back yard making it possible for us to watch the dogs as they did their business. When Clara ran around the corner of the house out of range of the spotlights, I followed her, discovering to my dismay that I couldn't see a thing. From the pitch blackness came a bark and then cries of pain. As my eyes became accustomed to the darkness I began to see Clara's black and brown coat. She was pawing at her mouth and wailing. Pulling her back into the lighted backyard, I could see her mouth was filled with porcupine quills. Zoe brought me pliers and I yanked seventeen quills from her tongue, mouth and muzzle.

Clara was a smart dog, but her hunting instinct could override her intelligence in a nanosecond. I'm sure, had there been another opportunity to attack a porcupine the next night, Clara would have done it. As soon as we were able, we had a five foot, horse wire fence plus split rails put up in the back yard. I cut a hole in the back door off the mud room, now the dog room, and inserted a dog door with a heavy vinyl flap. This allowed the dogs free access to the yard whenever they needed it. It also allowed the cold wintry winds easy access, but that's another story.

Clara was a dear dog despite her tendency to nip. She was Melanie's good friend and saw her though the difficult years of divorce, custody fight and chronic illness. In some ways Clara was an otherworldly dog, who, we liked to believe, could help us find lost items even after she died. Her mystical quality was explained when, in 1998, Zoe and I went to Egypt. Clara's nose, ears and body were identical to the pictures of the god dog, Anubis, as it sat atop sarcophagi. Eventually, Clara and Jamie negotiated a *rapprochement* that allowed a guarded friendship for the rest of Clara's life.

Zoe's not yet back from shopping and Jamie is sitting resolutely by the back door waiting for her return. I go to her and rub her ears, trying to distract her, but she won't move. When I sit on the floor beside her she lets me put my arms around her big head and hold her. I understand her devotion to Zoe. I feel the same way. Pretty soon she lies down and when I rub her belly she rolls onto her back like a puppy. I give her a good rough belly rub. When I stop she nudges my hand back to her belly for more rubbing. After a while she's content to put her head in my lap and let me rub her ears.

We always referred to Jamie as The Empress. She was the alpha dog in our pack, but lately she's the Empress Dowager. For the last year her daughter Bess has taken over the lead position which Jamie relinquished gracefully. In fact she's become quite mellow, partly from age and partly from Zoe's training. On walks she plods along beside Zoe, head down and swinging back and forth with the sway of her body. No longer does she attack pickup trucks as they drive by, nor tug at her leash, choking herself on the pinch collar to charge at another dog. Now she ignores the neighbors' dogs, so long as they keep their distance. She even tolerates the puppies when they mistake Gramma for their mommy.

Jamie, like me, has retired and seems to be enjoying life. She has had two litters of puppies, seven with Betty McDonnell and four with us. Out of her litters she produced six champions. Also with us she twice had puppies born dead. After the last two puppies were born dead two years ago we had her spayed.

"We're getting old," I say to Jamie, knuckling her ears and eliciting pleasurable moans. "Do you know that when Bess's puppies are ten years old, I'll be eighty-five. If we keep Mr. Orange, he's sure to weigh at least one hundred and sixty-five pounds. That's what I weigh now. At eighty-five, I'll probably weigh much less. Even now if Bess decides to lunge at the scent of a deer while we're walking, I can't hold her."

Jamie again moans ecstatically as I rub her ears.

"It's easy for you. We'll make sure you're fed and cared for. But what about me? I've got a hearing aid, a partial-plate, arthritis in my neck and back, a total hip replacement, and aortic stinosis in my heart valve. I'm getting old, Jamie. I'm wearing out. It scares me to think of keeping a potentially one hundred and sixty-five pound dog."

Jamie looks up at me with those big eyes that overflow with love and says, "It's never bothered you before. Just keep rubbing my ears. That's all that really matters."

The sound of the Astro's horn is heard as Zoe pulls into the driveway. Jamie and I meet her at the door, a switching tail wag from Jamie and a hug from me. I forget my worries and complaints. Our lives are complete again.

Chapter Seven

Patsy

*P*atsy's in heat. It started about the time the puppies were born. The first indication of the arrival of her season was her increasingly nutty behavior. She pranced about the dog yard sticking her butt in the other dogs' faces and occasionally mounting them. Zoe got the Kleenex tissue and rubbed her backend. "Yup," she said. "She's in heat." The tissue was stained red. She made an appointment with the vet for about a week later for a progesterone test which determines when a female is ready to be bred.

When Bear was still alive, in spite of his age he was better than a progesterone test. With Ellie, for instance, Bear knew when her time had come. Hobbling on his failing back legs, he would sidle up to her and somehow manage to mount her. Of course, there was nothing he could do when he got there, but his spirit was still willing to try. When Ellie shrugged him off, he would stand on wobbly legs and look at us from the dog yard. On his face was a broad smile of satisfaction that could give renewed hope to all the old farts of the world.

Patsy was one of three pups born to Ellie in 2003. That time of whelping was both joyous and sad. Jamie was pregnant and due about the same time as Ellie. I had built a second whelping box and we put both in the west wing so one of us could watch both sets of mothers and puppies at the same time. Ellie had her puppies and we waited expectantly for Jamie. But this was the time Jamie's puppies were born dead. I strung a sheet over Jamie's whelping box making a den, and Zoe rolled black stockings into balls and put them in the box. While the smell and sounds of Ellie's puppies nursing filled the west wing, Jamie would go into her whelping box and snuggle down with her rolled up stockings. It didn't last long, but for a few days it brought tears to our eyes and comfort to Jamie.

As Ellie's puppies grew, Melanie fell in love with Miss Red. We all did, for that matter. We sold two of the pups but kept Miss Red whom Zoe named Patsy Ketcham in honor of the dog given to her by her cousin, Ed Ketcham, when he left for the Navy in World War Two. For Valentine's Day, 2004, Zoe had Patsy's official AKC records changed to show co-ownership of Patsy with Melanie. The end of April, Zoe and Melanie took Patsy, Bess and Mattie to the Newfoundland National in Wisconsin. When they returned, Patsy wore a bright red collar trimmed in gold attached to a vibrant red leash, gifts from Melanie.

Patsy knows Melanie belongs to her. She sleeps in Melanie's room, sometimes on her bed. In the morning when Melanie wants to sleep in, she lets Patsy out of her room and shuts the door. Patsy tolerates this for about an hour, but then sits outside Melanie's door and barks for her to get up.

Patsy has by no means forgotten the rest of us. In the morning after the dogs and puppies have been fed, Zoe and I sneak back to bed for a cup of coffee and some reading. Ellie joins us and sprawls on the bed between us, while Mattie lies across Zoe, as limp as a cat, and lets Zoe rub her belly with her right hand while holding her book in her left. If she stops, Mattie paws at her book until she starts rubbing again. Patsy arrives and in one leap is on the bed. She stretches herself out on top of me and hugs me with her paws. I'm pinned to the mattress by her hundred and thirty pounds. Then come the kisses. If I'm lucky, I've removed my glasses in time because her face washing is thorough, covering my chin, cheeks, mouth, nose and eyes. There's no use pushing her away, which is impossible anyway, since she's going to keep kissing me until she's done. It lasts only about half a minute, then she gets up and moves over to Zoe for her turn.

I like to imagine that Patsy is proud of her

bark. Even when she was still a puppy she cultivated this basso profundo bark that sounded like a base tuba being played inside an enormous metal drum. When Bess sounds the alarm for a passing U.P.S. truck, Patsy picks up the alert with her booming barks, rallying all the dogs down to the play yard to defend the house. Sometimes, just to listen to the sound of her own voice, she will stand at the corner of the play yard and bark at nothing. At least that's what I thought she was doing until I heard the reverberations of her barking sounding off the walls of Pioneer Valley. I think she was barking to hear her echo.

On the day of the appointment, Melanie and I take Patsy to the vet where he draws blood for a progesterone test. The next day the lab sends back the results: 0.9. Two days later another test is 1.2. I don't know what this measures, but the vet says we'd better plan to have her bred in a couple of days. Meanwhile, Zoe and Melanie have been debating which dog should be the sire. Patsy's outstanding features are her marvelous head and loving eyes, but like her mother, Ellie, she is big for a Newfoundland female. Therefore a husky male, not too large, will make a good combination. The perfect sire is found down in New Jersey and Melanie and I take Patsy there for the breeding. The procedure to be used is artificial insemination, A.I. for short. Most breeders prefer A.I. because it prevents bacteria that might be in the female from infecting the male. At least, that's how I understand it. There are still a few breeders who prefer natural breeding, which is how I thought it was done before Zoe got into this business.

When I was an Episcopal priest, we had a dog named Barnabas, named after the mission church for which I was vicar. While we were waiting for our new church building to be constructed, we held Sunday School in the recreation room of our house. Barnabas was tied on a twenty foot chain in the yard outside the rec. room. The children liked Barnabas and liked watching him during Sunday School when he played with other dogs. One day a female dog came to visit him. The children hurried to the windows to watch. The female teased Barnabas by dancing back and forth just beyond the reach of the chain. Barnabas, the champion stud of the neighborhood, was no dope. He pretended to yank on the chain at approximately ten feet from where it was staked. When the female got closer and closer with her dance of the seven veils, suddenly Barnabas lurched to the full length of the twenty foot chain and nailed her.

"Mommy, Daddy," the children shouted as their parents picked them up after church, "guess what we learned today."

On another occasion, the fabled Barnabas fell in love one Christmas season with a dog belonging to one of the church members. Barnabas was a constant visitor at their house, howling at the front door for his girlfriend. When they refused to let her out, he tore the entire, elaborate string of Christmas lights off the front of the house and from around the garage door. I answered the phone to a voice trembling with suppressed anger. "Father, please come and get your dog."

So, artificial insemination, is new to me.

Once the semen has been collected from the male, I am given a chance to look at it under a microscope. Adjusting the focus for my eyes, I see about a million sperm, like tiny slivers, vibrating on the plate. I'm astounded. "Wow!" I exclaim, "and it only takes one."

When the procedure is completed, we're told to return in two days for another A.I., just to be sure.

Back home Zoe counts thirty days on the calendar and makes an appointment for Patsy to have a sonogram to see if she's pregnant. As we wait for the sonogram Melanie refuses to let herself even think about Patsy having puppies for fear it will jinx her. But on the morning of the day of the appointment, she can hardly contain her excitement. Zoe and Melanie leave with Patsy, plus Mattie, Ellie and Bess who will be seeing the vet for some tests. I stay home with Jamie and the puppies and take advantage of the sunny day to mow the lawn.

While they're gone, a nice thing happens. I finish the lawn, about a two hour job, and I'm hot and exhausted. Collapsing on the sofa I wait for my aortic stinosis to catch up with my body's need for blood. Jamie comes over and sticks her head in my face. I rub her ears, but am unable to induce the usual moan that Zoe gets from ear knuckling. Jamie thanks me for trying, then says, "Haven't you forgotten something?" Oh my goodness, I realize, it's three-thirty, one hour past her dinner time. I apologize and feed her.

To make up for my oversight, I ask, "How about a swim?" I put on my bathing suit and follow Jamie as she runs like a puppy to the gate that leads down to the river. She's already in the water when I get down the stone steps. The water is crystal clear and moving fast into the pool behind the ancient rock ledge that protrudes from our bank into the river. Sunlight coming through the overhanging branches patterns the rocky bottom with flickering shadows. Jamie dips her head in the water, then shakes it in a shiny swirl of droplets. Picking my way carefully over the slippery rocky bottom, I enter the pool. The water is cold so I decide only to wade. But the world has other plans. I misstep, lose my balance and fall over backward into the water. I'm soaking wet. Jamie comes to me delightedly wagging her tail.

"Just give yourself a good shake," she says, "like this." The shake starts with a violent wobble of her head producing a twisting spray of water, then moves down her back, ending with a wiggle of her butt and a wave of her tail. I decline the shake and instead hug her head and kiss her nose.

I think this is the first time Jamie and I have been alone together without Zoe and without the other dogs. It's good to rediscover what a sweetheart she is.

We hear the honking of the Astro in the driveway and hurry up from the river into the play yard. Melanie calls down to us. "She's pregnant! Patsy's pregnant. It looks like three and maybe four puppies."

Chapter Eight

For The Love Of Puppies

I'm so proud of the puppies. Not one has pooped during the night on the blanket in the X-pen. I open the dining room door to the dog yard, then to the X-pen, and they race to get out. No sooner are they in the yard then they take turns pooping. I get the scooper and follow them around.

"Let's get him," Miss Purple says and chases after me. Blue and Orange follow her. Purple grabs the right leg of my sweats and Blue and Orange the left. With their teeth securely locked into the fabric of my sweats, they dig their two inch wide paws into the pea stones and pull. I can't walk. These little puppies, at eight weeks old, have grown into monsters. They weigh more than eighteen pounds and stand a foot tall at their shoulders. Using all my strength I move one foot forward, then pull the other foot a step ahead. I'm making my way to a pile of poop when I realize my sweats are being pulled right off my behind. The puppies refuse to let go. Miss Purple starts shaking my leg like Clara used to do to break a skunk's neck. She's not strong enough to break my leg, but she does manage to pull my sweats down to my knees leaving me half-naked. With a lunge, I break free. Turning around I see the puppies, rolling on the ground, each pointing a paw at me and laughing uproariously, or so it seems.

There's no one who can see me, so why should I worry? At the back of our house beyond the dog yard is the Westfield River. On the other side of the river is a forest that stretches for miles. The houses on either side are two or three hundred feet away and not visible through thick stands of tall spruce. We're quite isolated.

Later that morning Zoe and I carry the puppies down the steps to the play yard. They love the grass and rock wall with its mysterious crevices. Miss Red dashes off across the lawn in search of something which she immediately forgets, and the others race after her, stopping to tackle one another along the way. The wood steps that lead down to the yard are a special delight. Mr. Blue hides under the steps and flashes out a paw at an unsuspecting and surprised Mr. Orange. Zoe and I watch the unending show for several happy moments, then lie down on the grass. Instantly six puppies are climbing over us, licking and nibbling on us. Taking Miss Purple in my hands and losing my fingers in her thick fur, I stare into her dark brown eyes, and kiss her nose. She squirms away, leaving me overflowing with love.

Back in the house, I'm writing at the computer in the study off the bedroom. The puppies and dogs have been fed, the X-pen cleaned out and folded against the wall, and Zoe's checking her mail on the computer in the family room. It's a time to relax for a moment, a catching up time.

I glance at a picture of Zoe in a little silver frame sitting on the hard drive. It was taken in 1950. She's seventeen, dressed in a sweater, blouse, and pleated skirt, and wearing a jacket. She leans casually on her left elbow, her back resting against a rock deep in the woods behind her house in Tarrytown, New York. She smiles at me and I'm with her again, tramping those woods, finding places of seclusion away from her parents and other people. It's summer vacation and each of us has two more years at the University of Chicago. During the summer Zoe's taking a secretarial course and I'm working as a plumber's helper at Anaconda Wire and Cable in Hastings on the Hudson. Every minute I'm not working, or sleeping at my boarding house in North Tarrytown, or on the bus to Tarrytown, I'm with Zoe.

We already plan to get married. It was on our second date the year before, that I, twenty years old, told Zoe, still sixteen, that I loved her and wanted to marry her. This summer we're driving her parents nuts with the intensity of our relationship.

"Just what are your intentions, young man?" her tall, handsome and very proper father says to me. Harold McKey is a vice president with the Norden Company. In World War One he was an army captain, wounded in France, and recipient of the *Croix de Guerre* and the Distinguished Service Cross for bravery.

"I intend to marry your daughter," I reply with the effrontery of youth.

"And when do you intend to do that?"

"When the time is right."

His eyes narrow, his lips grow tight. "And when is that?"

"I don't know right now. I will when the time comes," I say. The time came six months later when I received notice from the draft board for my pre-induction physical in January. The Korean War was in full swing. It was Christmas vacation. I was in Flint, Michigan with my folks, and Zoe was at her home in Tarrytown. We talked on the phone and decided to get married the end of January in case I got drafted. Our parents reluctantly agreed, mine knowing it wasn't worth it to argue with me, and Zoe's because I think they were afraid we needed to get married. I passed the physical, but was given a student deferment status. Zoe and I, much relieved, were married anyway and returned to the University of Chicago. I think

Harold and her mother, Marie, felt we'd put one over on them.

It wasn't until Harold retired and he and Marie moved to Tryon, North Carolina that I won his respect. One day when we were visiting with our three children, he showed me his 45 caliber pistol which he'd brought home from World War One. He'd taken it apart some years earlier and had never been able to put it back together. I had learned to field strip a 45 in the Navy so I was able to return it to its original working condition. He was impressed. Maybe I wasn't just some kid who'd stolen his daughter.

The jobs I held must have dismayed her parents. I'm sure Harold and Marie were upset that I never settled down to one thing. First it was the CIA, then the Navy, and then seminary and the Episcopal priesthood. Harold had died by the time I left the parish ministry, but her mother, Marie, lived to see me move into counseling, then real estate.

I wonder what they would think if they could see where we live now. To tell the truth, I think they'd love it. When they retired on the outskirts of Tryon they lived in a log house. Harold loved that place. He spent many hours in a little shed behind the house where he kept himself busy with his tools. One day he took our son Danny to a stream which ran down the heavily wooded hillside next to their house and showed him how to make a waterwheel. Marie, when she wasn't cooking marvelous meals for us, turned the sloping grounds at the front of the house into a lovely garden. Our big old house set in the seclusion of Pioneer Valley is not unlike the setting in which they chose to retire. But if Harold and Marie were to step inside our house, I'm sure they'd be aghast.

The living room's okay, in fact, quite respectable. There are rugs on the floor, three sofas and a chair, a coffee table with only one corner gnawed, books and items we've collected from our travels lining two walls, paintings by Robert, our grandson, and by our daughter, Melanie, on the remaining walls, and a pellet stove. The walls are painted a rich, dark green and the woodwork is white. This is where we entertain company and celebrate birthday parties. Generally we keep the door closed to the dogs except when we have a party.

All guests to our house are warned beforehand to dress in something that can withstand Newfie drool, because the dogs will want to greet them. Usually we bring guests into the house through the front door and usher them into the living room before we let the dogs in from the family room. Then the charge begins. The five dogs are so happy to see guests that they all crowd around them wanting to sniff and kiss them. Then they bound over to us to let us know we have guests, and we tell them we know, we invited them. Eventually, when everyone has found a seat, the dogs lie down and let us do the entertaining. If we're serving *hors d'oeuvres*, they're placed on the mantel of the fireplace where the dogs can only stare longingly. Our guests are warned to hold their drinks, because wagging Newfoundland tails are just the right height to sweep glasses off the coffee tables. A special tradition was started by old Bear for our birthday parties. As the cake is brought in, the dogs, with raucous barking, join with us in the singing of "Happy Birthday".

Apart from the living room, the rest of the house is pretty much shared equally with the dogs, and now, the puppies. The rugs, which we buy on sale for no more that $19.95, are rolled up because the puppies wander the house and, at eight weeks, are not housebroken. The original pine planks are well scratched by Newfie claws. The chairs and sofas, purchased from Goodwill or Salvation Army Resale, have gnawed arm rests and ripped upholstery with protruding stuffing. We cover these with blankets and throws. In the living room we use washable slip covers. When the furniture gets too disreputable, we throw it away and make another trip to the Salvation Army.

With puppies growing larger each day, their requirements change almost daily. Now, at night, they're in the X-pen which is set up each evening in the dining room and folded up in the morning. The dining room table has been moved to the family room in front of the new pellet stove. Already I have repaired the screen door in the dining room where the puppies tore open an escape route to the dog yard.

It's August so we leave the doors and windows open night and day. The puppies spend most of their time in the cool (a relative term given this summer's heat) of the metal roofed outdoor pen off the west wing shed. They stretch out in the shade on the cool moist pea stones and sleep. When the spirit moves them, or hunger pains arouse them, they poke their heads in the dining room door, then come into the house. They're like six big Teddy bears, soft and round with thick black fur. They express their love by chewing on whatever they can get hold of — pant legs, skirts, chin bones, fingers — and their teeth are sharp.

The big dogs go in and out through a new dog door I cut in the wall of the dog room. This is what's nice about an old house that's been a farm house, a home to the owner of the paper mill that used to be across the road, a boarding house and who knows what else over its two hundred year history. When we bought it, the west wing was an apartment which we wished to incorporate back into the house. Robert and I cut a hole in the separating wall removing hand sawed studs four inches square as well as horsehair plaster and stretched hemlock lathing. Then we framed it up and put in an old wooden door we found in the shed.

We may be nonchalant about our living relationship with the dogs, but our house is, nonetheless, fairly clean. It's vacuumed daily, the floors are scrubbed once a week or more, the kitchen is straightened and the counters washed after every meal, and the dog yard sprayed with Clorox twice a week. That doesn't mean there isn't Newfie drool on the ceiling or dog hair on a recently vacuumed rug over which one of the dogs has walked. Immaculate is not a word that goes with a house in which Newfoundlands live.

Last July after the puppies were born, one of my college roommates, Verne Henderson, and his wife, Kiki, dropped by for lunch. We warned them that our dogs considered themselves a welcoming committee for all visitors, and that the house belonged to the dogs as much as to us. They laughed and said,

"Sure," as if we were being facetious. Zoe and I have been to their home in Brookline and know it to be eloquently decorated with a place for everything and everything in its place. So it was understandable when they walked in and exclaimed, "You guys are crazy. This isn't your house. It really does belong to the dogs." Yet, they did fall in love with the puppies.

We weren't offended at their comment, first, because we love Verne and Kiki, and second, because we agree. There's a kind of creeping disease Zoe and I have called Newflovitis that started when we got Jamie. As we acquired more Newfoundlands, we didn't realize how the disease was taking its toll on us. When callers come into the house I would be willing to bet they smell dogs, although I no longer smell them. When they sit on the sofa and find dampness oozing through their pants into their underwear, they are probably annoyed. We apologize for not telling them that Ellie had been lying there when she came in from a swim in the river. Seeing Mattie chewing the legs of our dining room chairs, they might say, "You mean you let her do that?"

"Oh yes," we say. "You should see what she's done to the rungs on the upstairs banister."

I took Verne and Kiki for a tour of the

house showing off the new closet I built off the study and the replastering job I did to repair the walls of the study damaged by roof leaks. We returned to the family room where Zoe was reading the paper and drinking a glass of water. Picking our way through the dogs who were sprawled on the floor, we settled down. As we talked, Ellie walked over to Zoe and began to drink from her glass.

Kiki shouted, "Zoe, the dog's got her nose in your glass."

Zoe glanced over. "Ellie, you've got your own water. Leave mine alone." Ellie raised her head and backed off.

The conversation continued until Kiki cried, "Zoe, you're drinking out of that glass."

"Oh," Zoe said, "I hadn't noticed. So I am."

That's what I mean about Newflovitis. It's a silent, sneaky disease that eventually insinuates itself into every corner of your life. But where some diseases are debilitating, Newflovitis is invigorating.

An enormous truck arrived as Verne and Kiki were leaving. After we said good bye, I turned my attention to the truck which was delivering our pellets for the new stove. There were three pallets each stacked with 2400 pounds of pellets. That's 180 bags which should last us for most of the winter. The driver revved up the engine, swung out the hydraulic crane, attached the fork lift, and deftly unloaded each pallet, wrapped in light blue shrinkwrap, onto the driveway.

When he replaced the hydraulic crane and turned down the engine, he noticed the five Newfoundlands who had come into the play yard to supervise the unloading.

"What are those dogs?" he asked. "They look like bears."

"They're called Newfoundlands."

"You raise them?"

"My wife does," I said. "I help."

"You sell them?"

"That's right."

"Make any money at it?"

I laughed. "Nope. We don't even break even."

He shook his head and turned toward the cab of the truck. "Why do you do it then?"

After a moment's pause, I said, "I think for the love of puppies — especially Newfoundland puppies."

He nodded. "Makes sense. I got a mutt. Got him when he was a pup. Cutest thing. Grown up now. I love him still. But there's nothing like a pup."

Chapter Nine

Danger in Paradise

"What a wonderful place to live," the man calls to me from the road. He's middle aged and dressed for the August heat in a sport shirt and shorts. I'm clipping dead Geranium flowers to make room for new ones around the stone steps leading to our front door.

"Thank you." I stand, stretch my back, then cross the yard to the rail fence next to the road. "Are you here on vacation?" I know he doesn't live around here, because I know everyone who does, if not by name, at least by looks. When Zoe and I are walking the dogs, we wave at approaching cars and pickup trucks most of which we recognize. Behind the tinted glass we just make out a hand waving back. At first I was selective in my waving, only to the cars I recognized. When I noticed Zoe waving at a guy in an unfamiliar pickup truck, I asked if she knew him. "No," she said, "I wave at everybody in case I should know them." So I, too, started greeting all the cars.

"Not really a vacation," the man says. "I'm down at the Remington Lodge. Brought our high school gymnastics club out here to go rafting on the Deerfield River. I'm the coach."

"It should be good. We've had lots of rain."

"That," he says, "and they open the flood

gates so there's plenty of water." He knows more about it than I do. "We're from Needham over near Boston." He lets his eyes rove slowly down the full length of the rail fence that runs along the front of our property. "You're lucky to live out here," he says. I infer from his wistful expression that he's seeing not only through his eyes but through some bucolic vision of the perfect place to live. "It's so peaceful and quiet."

I say that we really like living here and wish him good rafting. He continues ambling down the road and I return to the front steps, pick up the Geranium clippings and head around back. Rob, our artist grandson, is kneeling in the dog yard, taking pictures of the puppies with his new digital camera. Two puppies are frozen in mid-charge directly at the camera. Another is caught in an enormous yawn. One puppy has both paws in the drinking dish as if to hold it down while he laps water. These pictures, along with about a thousand others, are filed in the computer. Some are selected to rotate through a puppy slide show. I sit in the shade of the house and watch.

Kreech, kreech. What a strange screeching sound. Rob hears it too. We look around but see nothing out of the ordinary. *Kreech, kreech.* We hear it again. "I know that sound," Rob says. "It's a hawk. Look! Up there." I look straight up. Circling far above us is a huge hawk. It continues its eerie screeching. *Kreech, kreech.* As it circles over us, it comes lower and lower. The six puppies are chasing each other around the dog yard.

"My God!" I shout. "I think it's after the puppies."

"Sure looks like it," Rob says, studying the soaring raptor.

"What kind is it?"

"It looks like a red tailed hawk."

"Would it be big enough to pick up a puppy?"

Rob knows a lot about birds. He says, "Some have a twenty-five inch wing span. If it couldn't snatch a pup, it could still do a lot of damage." We walk out into the yard and stand in the midst of the puppies who come over and start tugging on our shoe laces. "Think I could get it with the potato cannon?" Rob asks.

A word needs to be said about the potato cannon. It's a gift from our grandson William to his cousin McKey who is currently in Marblehead as assistant director with the Rebel Shakespeare Company. The cannon is eight feet long and consists of a five foot barrel made of two inch PVC pipe. This is connected to a three foot piece of four inch PVC which acts as an explosion chamber. An electric spark device is strapped to the explosion chamber and can be activated by pushing a button. To fire the cannon, a potato is ramrodded down the barrel and an underarm deodorant is sprayed into the explosion chamber. Quickly, a cap is screwed tight on the end of the chamber. The cannon is aimed, the button is punched and the deodorant explodes. The potato is fired five or six hundred feet straight up or for a distance of at least seven hundred and fifty feet on a graceful ballistic curve.

When most of the grandchildren are here, usually with a collection of their friends, we invite the old guys of the neighborhood to come over for the shooting of the cannon. They watch the youngsters with old man skepticism.

The cannon is readied. Our grandsons suggest that our neighbors step back. They chuckle to themselves, but to please the boys they move back a foot or two. Then William, the designer and engineer of the cannon, pushes the button.

WHAM!

"God Almighty!" shouts Bill Volk, our resident lawyer, architect and balloonist. Others are equally awestruck. The potato sails out across the Westfield River and hundreds of feet away into the woods. "What the hell did you squirt into that thing?" Bill asks.

"Underarm deodorant," William says.

Bill guffaws, "I'm getting me some of that stuff."

As we gaze up at the hawk, Rob and I seriously consider hauling out the potato cannon, when we notice the hawk is drifting off. I guess our very presence among the puppies has caused it to reconsider the risk of diving into the dog yard.

We do live in the wilds. Animals visit us often. Zoe, Melanie and the boys see them, but I'm never around when they come. We've been living here five years and it's not fair that I'm the only one who has seen nothing but a deer or two. One day a fully grown moose with a rack of antlers walked down our street in front of the house. Another time I was coming home in the van when I saw our next door neighbor, George Racz, standing in our driveway waving at me excitedly. "You just missed it," he shouted. "A big bear, maybe three, four hundred pounds, was in the dogs' play yard. He crossed the yard, jumped the fence and went down to the river." I ran into the house with the news. Zoe was in the kitchen and Melanie was resting in her room. They hadn't seen a thing. Our mighty guard dogs were all sound asleep in the family room. When I called them to come to the play yard they went wild, racing back and forth along the fence, sniffing every step the bear had taken. We now have a plaster cast which Melanie made of the bear's foot. I don't know what would have happened had the dogs been in the play yard to meet the bear, but it would have been ugly.

The woods around us are filled with prey and predator. About half the cheery bird calls are not so cheery. They're robins defending their nests from blue jays, sparrows fending off crows, merganser ducks protecting their babies from marauders. In hunting season, the sound of occasional gun fire lets us know it's time to strap red scarfs on our bear-sized dogs when we go walking.

Two winters ago five wild turkeys spent a lot of time in the yard across the street. They're a pretty bird, much more attractive than a domesticated turkey. I can see why Ben Franklin thought they would make a good national bird instead of the bald eagle. One morning I found one lying in the road, hit by a car.

When five o'clock comes I sit with Rob by the dog fence above the river. The sun has settled behind the trees, flooding the yard with shade. Zoe and Melanie join us and listen to the story of the puppies and the red tailed hawk. Zoe worries. Anything threatening her puppies or her dogs is an anathema. We realize that we must be on our guard all the time, not only for things we can imagine, like a visiting bear, but for things we haven't even thought of.

I sip my scotch, Zoe her black Russian, Rob his wine and Melanie her root beer. It's a quiet time at the end of the day. The puppies mill about our shoes, nibbling our shoe laces, trying to knock over our drinks, chewing on corners of the *Hampshire Gazette*, looking up at us with their dark brown eyes and asking to be petted. The sound of the river rushing over rocks creates our own *Water Music*. Gradually our anxiety over the hawk evaporates into the soft evening breeze.

The gymnastic coach is right. This is a peaceful place. So, there are occasional dangers. Even the Garden of Eden had its snake.

In the distance I hear the guttural call of our neighborhood raven. He lives with his mate under the bridge out on Highway 9 in a huge nest of sticks and leaves. I say our raven, because he's been here as long as we have. Sometimes when we're walking the dogs he flies down the road only a few feet above our heads just to let us know how really big he is. His beak looks like a pickax, and his wing span is at least three feet. Now, as we sit in the dog yard, the sound of his call grows louder. Suddenly he appears over the roof of the house. He's hot on the tail of a hawk — the same red tailed hawk? — which is swooping, diving and making vain attempts to flip sideways in order to catch the raven in its talons. As they pass overhead it's like watching two World War One airplanes dog fighting in the sky. The raven's persistent pursuit eventually drives the hawk to the far side of the river where I think it lives.

Moments later the raven returns victorious. As a salute to us, he dips his wings and we cheer, or maybe I imagine this part.

Chapter Ten

Waltzing Mathilda

*F*or all of us who sometimes feel we don't belong, Waltzing Mathilda's been there too. For those of us who try hard to be accepted, but more often than not screw up, Waltzing Mathilda's a pro. And for those of us who fight for our rightful share but get in trouble doing so, Waltzing Mathilda says, "Tell me about it". Yes, there's a little bit of all of us in Waltzing Mathilda.

Mathilda, at thirteen months, is smaller than the other dogs and not as heavy. Her nose is straighter without the Newfie wrinkles. When she's in coat, she's beautiful with abundant feathers and a full chest. But out of coat, like now, she looks like a waif blown in from the storm. Also, she's in heat, and constantly backing up to the other female dogs begging them to help her out, but not sure what that means. We won't help by finding her a big handsome male, because she's still too young.

A year ago when we could get neither Bess nor Ellie pregnant after the second try, Zoe decided to buy a puppy. Robin Seamen had two sired by a champion dog named Merlin. We watched them in their pen and decided on the one with the most attitude. She could be a champion for sure. With a father like Merlin, Zoe thought a magical name would be appropriate for the puppy. She turned to a movie made a few years ago about a little girl named Mathilda who could do magic. But the name Magic Mathilda didn't seem to fit. Then Zoe's long love affair with Australia, a place she still hasn't visited, made her think of the song, *Waltzing Mathilda*, and that was that. In the evening when we're reading in bed, Mathilda, limp as a boneless cat, sprawls across Zoe's stomach, while Zoe rubs her tummy and sings *Waltzing Mathilda*.

Mattie was three months old when we brought her home. She came into a house where there were two mother-daughter sets; Jamie and Bess, and Ellie and Patsy. The hierarchical order was well established. Jamie, the Empress, was boss, and Bess was the Princess. Ellie was the spokesperson for the pack, for instance, letting us know when it was time to eat. Patsy was a year old and still full of herself. Mathilda was just puppy enough to be tolerated by the other dogs so long as she kept her place. But Mattie wanted to play with the big dogs and she wanted more than her share of chewy treats when Zoe handed them out. Growls from the older dogs should have told Mattie to respect her elders, but for Mattie the reprimands were a challenge. The first feeding time was a disaster. Zoe put the bowls down for the other dogs who were accustomed to eating next to each other. To be safe, she fed Mattie in the family room. But Mattie finished in a split second and charged into the dog room sticking her nose into the other dogs' bowls. She ignored the growls and nipping and started fighting back. A brawl ensued and we intervened with whiffle bats. For several weeks after that, Mattie was fed in the family room with the door closed to the dog room.

Now at thirteen months Mattie attempts to emulate Bess as Guardian of Homeland Security. It hasn't gone well. During the summer, cross-country skiers keep in shape with short skies on wheels. The dogs know they're coming by the clicking of their ski poles on the asphalt road. Bess runs to the front door and barks vociferously through the screen. Mattie, not to be outdone, leaps onto the desk in the family room barking wildly through the open window. She tips the I-Mac computer precariously, scatters papers, knocks off the pencil sharpener and almost sends the scanner airborne. Instead of praise for bravery, she gets a good scolding.

And how many times, when the other dogs are snug in the family room with us during a storm, have I looked out and seen Mattie sitting in the corner of the play yard, her coat matted with rain, looking forlornly down the road as if waiting for a friend. When I go out to get her, she runs to me, tail wagging and says for the hundredth time, "You do love me, don't you?"

Mattie's struggles to find her place in our house came to a head one day when, either deliberately or inadvertently, she snatched a chewy treat from Jamie, the Empress. Jamie snapped back and in an instant Mattie had Jamie's jowl locked in her teeth and wouldn't let go, probably because she knew Jamie would kill her if she did. The growling and snarling was deafening. The other dogs joined in, leaping about and barking at the combatants. We tried whiffle bats but to no avail. We yanked on Mattie's rear, but she refused to let go. Finally Zoe dumped a whole pail of water mixed with vinegar on their heads and we managed to separate them. Still Mattie tried to break free to charge at Jamie. I pulled Mattie into the front hall and shut the door. Zoe comforted Jamie whose lip was torn and bleeding.

When tempers cooled Mattie couldn't apologize enough to Jamie. She licked Jamie's eyes and mouth until Jamie said, "Enough already." But something had happened in the order of things. Jamie was actually cautious around Mattie, either because she considered the puppy unpredictable or she was willing to relinquish her command. Whatever it was, Bess became top dog and Jamie settled into a position of alpha emeritus. For Mattie, Jamie has become a good friend. Every morning she washes Jamie's face and licks night goo from her eyes. And Jamie seems to like it.

When I see Waltzing Mathilda sitting at the end of the play yard all by herself, I see myself standing by the country club pool as a twelve year old. Bruce Stewart had invited me to the pool for the afternoon and was busy diving and swimming. I knew I didn't belong there. I couldn't dive. I didn't swim well. But most of all, these were the rich kids and I wasn't one of them. My skinny legs were shivering under my sagging wool bathing suit. I was sure the other kids, especially the girls, were laughing at me, and they probably were. How I wanted that day to end.

After sixty-three years, the sight of Mattie all alone at the end of the play yard still brings back a flood of old feelings.

I don't know how important mother-daughter relationships are among dogs, but I think Mattie feels like an outsider around the other four dogs. In the morning after everyone is fed, sometimes Zoe and I go back to bed for coffee and reading. Mattie joins us and, sitting between us, puts her paw on my arm asking to be petted. She looks at us wistfully with partially closed eyes that seems to say, "Do you really love me?" I pet her back and Zoe rubs her tummy. Again the paw comes out and she asks. "Will you keep me always?" I raise my head to her and she tongues a polite little kiss on my cheek. "Of course we love you Mattie." And Zoe says, "You're our Waltzing Mathilda."

When I transferred to the University of Chicago from the University of Michigan, I lived with Verne Henderson and Dick Deising in Robie House, the famed Frank Lloyd Wright house. We shared what had been the maid's quarters above the double garage. The rest of the house was occupied by married students. Zoe and I began serious courting as soon as I came to Chicago, and she was a frequent visitor to the maid's quarters, as were the girlfriends of Verne and Dick. The house still had all the original Frank Lloyd Wright furniture which now must be worth a fortune in some museum. In front of the huge fieldstone fireplace was a wide sofa which the three of us couples reserved on a sign up sheet. Zoe and I, every third night, built a fire and curled up on the sofa to study. Uh huh.

I lived with Verne and Dick crammed into two small rooms, but I didn't feel like I was one of them. Their talk centered around the deep psychological implications of everything they said to each other, and frankly I felt left out. I wish I could have said that I didn't give a damn, but at the time I felt I lacked their sensitivity and understanding. Like Mattie with the other four dogs, I felt like an outsider. It wasn't a pleasant feeling.

As a parish priest, the structure of the priest-parishioner relationship perpetuated my feelings of being an outsider. A minister comes into a congregation which was there before he or she arrived and will be there after he or she leaves. They are your flock and you do your best to love them as you minister to their needs. But close friendships are a rarity. I think the congregation wants it this way, because as their priest you know many intimate details about each of them, and it could make them uneasy if you were too close to one or two other members. In any case, this structure fit my sense of being an outsider. Still, it was accompanied by the tinge of loneliness that comes with being separate.

In the last few years, however, I have come to realize that my feelings of not belonging are something I put on myself; not only in the different jobs I've had or the places we've live, but even in my own family. It's taken me seventy-five years, but finally I'm beginning to know and believe that I am loved by my family and accepted as an integral part. It must be a great relief to Zoe who has had to bear the strains that my outsider feelings put on our relationship. On the occasions when these feeling of loneliness occur, and they still do from time to time, I know they are generated from within and not imposed from the outside. I am not that skinny little kid in the wool bathing suit shivering at the edge of the country club pool. I'm a member of a wonderful and loving family. I enjoy being a grandfather, and am proud of the accomplishments of all our grandchildren as artist, actor, costume designer, fencer, archer, singer, film maker, sojourner and karate student. Melanie lives with us, and our other children, Daniel and Martha, are not far away. I am beginning to learn that I can turn to them for help when needed, which is another avenue toward bridging separation.

Waltzing Mathilda, like me, is beginning to find her place in our family of humans and Newfoundlands. She taught the other dogs how to jump the fence in the play yard, until I made the fence taller. She takes care of Jamie in her declining years whether Jamie likes it or not. For the most part Jamie likes it. And with Bess's puppies, Mattie has become their nursemaid. She leads them around the dog yard showing them how to play soccer, how to chew the sprigs of grass along the fence and how to play tug-of-war with the blanket drying out on the fence.

This morning I took Mattie with me in the car to get the paper. As she sat on the seat feeling privileged to go in the car, I told her I love her and that we'll never let her go. She looked out the window at the passing scene, then leaned her head over backward and gave me a kiss.

Chapter Eleven

Two Seasons

*O*ur 180 bags of pellets wrapped in light blue shrinkwrap and stacked on three pallets, sit in our driveway looking exactly like three port-o-pots. They weigh a total of 7200 pounds. The question is, how do I get them into the barn? Each of the last three years I ordered five cord of firewood for our two wood stoves to supplement the thousand dollars worth of oil we bought for our two furnaces. If you know firewood, five cord can take up most of a good sized driveway. Thanks to grandchildren William, James, Rachel and McKey we got it stacked in the barn before the snow blew. Because it was an unpleasant task, I paid them. This year I am looking for an easier and perhaps cheaper way to get the forty pound bags into the barn. Also, McKey is in New York attending the American Academy of Dramatic Arts and Rachel is attending Berkshire Community College. Since it's too big a job for William alone, even with twelve year old James's help, I look elsewhere for a way.

Asking around I discover that Bob Aeschback, up West Road behind Deer Hill, has a fork lift, and he agrees to put the pallets in the barn for fifty dollars. He arrives with a tractor so big that only the forks can fit into the barn. But he's clever. He sets one pallet in the door way, then pushes it to the back of the barn with the next pallet. The third pallet he sets just inside the doors, blocking them so they won't close. These bags will have to be relocated by hand. But at least, all three are under roof.

As he's getting ready to leave, Bob quips, "They say we have only two seasons in New England: winter and getting ready for winter." In the five years we've been here, I've come to understand what he means.

Last winter we had several mornings when the thermometer shivered at more than twenty below zero. I would go downstairs at four-thirty or five, start the coffee and build a fire in our wood stove in the family room, now replaced with a pellet stove. Soon cheery flames would flicker in the stove and I'd settle down on the sofa with a good book and five black dogs to keep me company. Both McKey and Rob were away at college except during Christmas vacation, so I didn't have to turn up the oil heat in the west wing where they stay when they're here. The oil furnace for the rest of the house wouldn't be turned up from fifty-two to sixty-two until Zoe and Melanie got up. One room, the family room, was kept warm with the wood stove.

The dogs loved it. Even as cold as it got at night, they'd sprawl in the upstairs hall, lying on their backs, feet in the air, exposing their light pink hairless bellies. If it snowed during the night, as it often did, we'd hear the town's snowplow about three in the morning screeching its blade on the asphalt, and see its revolving light flashing across our bedroom wall. At first light, I'd get out the snowblower, clear snow which the plow had piled three feet deep at the front of the driveway and against the roadside gate to the play yard. Then I'd push the snowblower into the play yard and dig a moat around the inside of the entire fence. The first year I didn't do this and the dogs walked right over the top of the buried four foot fence. And last year, six month old Mattie discovered she could stand on a hill of snow and leap across the three foot moat into the road. So I added another foot to the top of the fence using two-by-fours.

Bess, Patsy and Mattie loved a fresh snow, the deeper the better. They kangaroo-leaped across the deep snow chasing each other, burying their heads in the snow and throwing muzzle loads into the air. Sometimes Ellie got into the chase, but Jamie preferred to observe from the bottom of the steps. Zoe brought home a huge blue ball from Wal-Mart and tossed it into the yard. Mattie was onto it in a flash, pursuing it around the moat like the driver of a luge. When she cornered it, she climbed on top, her four legs barely touching the ground, and proclaimed, "I win."

Bess and Patsy had marvelous "fights" with fangs flashing, guttural growls and fisticuffs while standing on their back legs. Mattie, in spite of her age, would dive into the fray with a body block knocking over both of them. The dogs would become so covered with snow that they looked like the white and black Newfoundlands called Landseers.

We managed the twenty degrees below zero pretty well in our warm family room, but when the wind blew, and it does, the cold would come through and around all of the thirty-one, two hundred year old windows. Our living room was used only when we were willing to burn our precious oil. A fire in the living room fireplace looked nice, but it warmed only the backside of whomever was sitting on the hearth right in front of it. Mid-January, Zoe came up with the idea of putting a pellet stove in the living room. It was expensive, but it allowed us to expand beyond the crowded family room.

A pellet stove burns capsule sized pellets made of pressed hardwood sawdust. Thus, it's recycling a byproduct of the lumber industry. An electric auger delivers a controlled amount of pellets to a fire box, the amount depending on how much heat is wanted. The exhaust is blown up through an existing chimney in a stainless steel pipe. The placing of this pipe through our thirty foot chimney in mid-January was a problem. There was at least a foot or two of snow on the roof. I know better than to go onto our roof in the summer, and wouldn't dream of it in the winter. I called our chimney sweep, who agreed to do the job. Drawing on his hobby of rock climbing, he used all his ropes, connectors and expertise to scale the snow covered roof.

With oil prices skyrocketing, this summer we decided to buy a second pellet stove and insert it into the fireplace in the family room, replacing the wood stove. Hence the purchase of all the pellets. This winter we should be able to get by with using much less oil. The only disadvantage of the pellet stove over the wood stove is its dependence on electricity. The year before we moved here they had an ice storm that cut electrical service for three days. If this happens again, we'll all move into the west wing where we still have a wood stove.

It is now September and dark as night when we feed the puppies and dogs at six in the morning. I turn on the flood lights in the dog yard, throw open the dining room and the X-pen doors. The puppies rush out. Immediately they grab the legs of my sweats and start pulling. It seems more than a game. I think they're pissed off at having been stuck in the pen all night. And when their teeth cut into the flesh of my legs, I think they're also hungry. They weigh well over twenty pounds each and with all of them attached to my legs, that's a one hundred and twenty pound anchor. Holding up my sweats with one hand I pry their teeth away with the other, then struggle to a chair next to the fence. It's like wading through a shark infested sea. Once I'm standing on the chair they lose interest and turn to the more pressing issue of peeing. Soon Zoe arrives at the dining room door with their three pans of food and they rush to the outdoor pen where they're shut in for breakfast. While they eat I remove the pee soaked and poop smeared blankets from the X-pen, hang them on the fence and hose them down. Then I fold up the X-pen. Later Zoe will mop the floor. When the puppies and the big dogs finish eating, I open the gate to the outdoor pen. The puppies tumble out to play in the dog yard. Eventually they find their way into the house through the dining room door which we leave open most of the day. When they pee and occasionally poop in the house, we wipe it up. After all, they're still puppies and not housebroken.

We could leave them in the outdoor pen night and day. I built it as a dog run with a door that goes inside the shed to a cozy enclosure which can even be kept warm in winter with a heat lamp. We wouldn't have puppies under foot, running through the house chewing on the sofa and chairs, and we wouldn't have to wipe up puppy pee puddles. Other people do it this way. It would be easier, but it would also defeat the whole purpose of having puppies. We could neither see their ridiculous antics nor ruffle their soft fur as they climb into our laps.

Every time I open the refrigerator door, two puppies squeeze in to investigate this marvelous container of good smells. I take what I want with one hand, pull back puppy heads with the other and close the door with my shoulder. As I slice bacon for breakfast, six sets of pleading eyes look up at me, just hoping. Loading the dishwasher requires unloading at least two puppies from the lower rack every time I put in a dirty plate. And when the pains of arthritis make me think it's time to give up, Miss Red sticks her head in an empty oatmeal carton and runs across the kitchen. Pain and discouragement give way to laughter and I know I can survive. When I sit down for one more cup of coffee and the morning paper, Mr. Orange climbs into my lap, puts his head in the crook of my arm and falls asleep. Who wanted to read the paper anyway? I set it aside and let my fingers dig into the soft bundle of fur in my lap.

Signs of fall and harbingers of winter are everywhere. As I clean up after the dogs in the dog yard, I realize I am constantly fooled by the increasing quantity of brown leaves on the ground that look a lot like poop. I stop to gaze across the river into the woods and am able to see trees and rocks that had been hidden by thick foliage only days ago. The leaves have drawn into themselves like old people hunching their shoulders against the cool nights. One or two branches at the tops of trees high on Deer Hill have turned a brilliant red. We see woolly caterpillars on the road as we walk the dogs. Driving home from the grocery store in Pittsfield I catch sight of a line of Canada geese flying high across a field of cut and baled hay.

When we still lived in the condo in Boston before moving to Marblehead, our contact with nature was a walk through the Public Garden. There was one tree with a hollow about twenty feet up the trunk. One day I spotted a squirrel looking at me from the hollow. As winter came, I liked to imagine that little squirrel hunkered down in the hollow, snug in a nest of leaves, protected from the rain and snow. It takes only a chill in the air to cause me to look for a hollow myself. Like the black bears up in the woods, I begin to prepare my shelter for the winter that's just around the corner.

This year it's buying new windows to replace the old ones that rattle when the wind blows. They are thermopane windows that we hired a carpenter to insert into the existing frames. To save money, I painted all sixty-two sashes of the double-hung windows. Now they're in place. The pellets are in the barn. There's fresh lubricating oil in the snowblower. All that remains before the winter winds blow down the valley shaking our old house is to enjoy walking the dogs under the beautiful fall leaves.

Chapter Twelve

A Critical Exam

*I*t takes balls to be a show dog, unless we're talking about female dogs. And it takes a good heart and mouth too. Two years ago when we took Jamie's four puppies to the cardiologist for the second month examination, one of the hearts was questionable, one had somewhat of an overbite, and one of the males had only one testicle. The puppies with the overbite and heart problem outgrew them and became champions, but the one with only half his maleness could never be a show dog. This doesn't mean he was any less lovable. He grew up to be a wonderful pet.

As we near the time for Bess's puppies to make the trip down to the veterinarian cardiologist in Connecticut, our household grows anxious. The disappointment we felt over Jamie's puppies that didn't pass part of the exam is still fresh in our minds. This year there's an added concern. We want to keep a female and a male as part of our expanding family, and we hope to show them. Also, Zoe has told Rob that he can be co-owner of the male, and McKey, co-owner of the female. We will choose what we feel are the best male and female of the litter because we want to breed them when they come of age. But our options are already reduced by two: Mr. White whose tail is bobbed, and Miss Purple with the kink at the base of her tail.

And there's one other problem. Miss Red and Mr. Orange have already decided they want to live with us. Miss Red is smart and she's a leader. She's the first of the puppies to figure out how to open the new hinged dog door that replaced the one with the vinyl flap. Sitting by the door she watches Mattie go in, then gets up on her back feet, pushes the spring-loaded door open and walks into the dog room. Zoe, in the kitchen, calls out to me, "I thought you were going to keep them in the dog yard until I feed the big dogs."

"I am. The door's closed."

"Well, Miss Red's in here, helping me."

It isn't long before Miss Red is leading a contingent of puppies through the dog door and into the house. This means I'll have to put the puppies in their outdoor pen when we feed the big dogs.

Miss Red was also first to climb into the dishwasher when we're filling it, the first to climb onto the sofa, the first to brave four steps of the stairs, and the first to wrench a large section of upholstery from the recliner chair. She has decided this is her house and she'll use it as she sees fit.

McKey decided that he was partial to Miss

Red when he returned from his job with the Rebel Shakespeare Company in Marblehead. Before he left for New York he would hold Miss Red on his lap and explain that she will be named Ros, for Rosalind in *As You Like It*.

But what if she doesn't pass the exam?

Mr. Orange doesn't care much about learning new things. This morning I notice that he remains by the dining room screen door waiting for someone to let him in while Miss Red leads the other puppies through the dog door. Still, he has decided that Zoe, Melanie, McKey and I, and especially Rob, belong to him. In the morning he not only grabs my sweats in his mouth, he also clutches me with his front legs. In the evening when we're having cocktails by the fence in the dog yard he's the one trying to get into our laps to be held. He's the largest of the puppies, very macho in his stance and proud in his walk. Before Rob left to return to the University of Hartford, he fell in love with Mr. Orange. The two of them were often seen in the yard, Mr. Orange curled up in Rob's lap. Mr. Orange assumes that we are his family and he waits only for us to acknowledge it.

But what if he doesn't pass the exam?

We take all six puppies to Jane Thibault and Zoe asks her to inspect Mr. Orange to see if he has two testicles. "Well, I can find one, but maybe it's too early for the second one." Zoe sighs. Kathy Luce comes by to see the puppies and Zoe asks her to feel for testicles. Kathy holds Mr. Orange upside down and probes his groin. "There's one for sure," she says, "but every time I touch him, he sucks 'em up and I can't find them." Again Zoe sighs.

What will we do if we have to choose two puppies other than Red and Orange? How will we ever be able to tell the boys?

There's a world of hope riding on our trip to the cardiologist. The puppies are in three crates, two to a crate, and Mattie, who is going for her one year heart exam is sitting between Zoe and me taking full advantage of two hands to pet her. Mattie will also have an identification chip inserted under her skin that will remain there all her life. A special meter reads the I.D. number that only Mattie will have.

The one hundred and seven mile trip is an adventure in itself since we have to drive through the pouring rain of tropical storm Francis that so devastated Florida. Still we are on time with one minute to spare.

Newspapers are put on the floor of one of the exam rooms and a baby gate is stretched across the doorway. Zoe and I carry the puppies in one at a time and dump them over the gate. Then Zoe brings Mattie in and puts her in the room also. When Zoe leaves the waiting room to get something from the van, Mattie, perhaps fearful she's being left behind, leaps the baby gate knocking it over and chases after her. Instantly, the puppies see the unbarred door of the exam room and run out into the waiting room finding several new places to pee. I manage to catch Mattie at the outside door just as a terrified women is bringing her cat into the office. Fortunately, Mattie isn't interested in the cat. She just wants to go with Zoe. Finally we put Mattie in one of the crates in the van where she lies down. "Thank you," she seems to say, "for getting me out of that mad house."

Her reprieve is only temporary because the vet wants to see her first. He declares her heart to be in fine condition and inserts the chip using a very large hypodermic needle. "Now for the puppies," the vet says.

We return Mattie to a crate in the van and bring in Miss Red, placing her on the metal topped exam table. Her feet are unsteady on the slippery table and she stands motionless with her head down not looking at anyone. The doctor asks, "Has she been well?"

"Yes," we both say at the same time.

"Is she active? Does she run and play with the other puppies."

"Very much so," Zoe replies. I want to tell him how smart she is and how she's a leader, but I decide he doesn't need to know all that.

He comes over to the table and, holding her head in his hands, tells her how beautiful she is. Then he whispers some comforting words in her ears. Miss Red raises her head and looks at him with an expression that says, "I guess you're okay."

With a flashlight he looks into her eyes, then pulls back her lips and examines her gums, teeth and bite. I'm dying for a comment as to her bite, but he says nothing to me, speaking only in a gentle voice to Miss Red. Moving his hands along her belly he twists his wristwatch so he can see it, then finds a place, maybe in her back legs, where he takes her pulse. Next comes the stethoscope which he holds against her chest, first on one side, then on the other. The room is in total silence. At one point he holds her mouth closed to stop her from panting, I guess so he can hear her heart beats without air moving into the lungs. He finishes, asking us to hold her so she doesn't fall off the table, and moves to his computer.

I look at Zoe, my expression asking, "When is he going to tell us?" But he doesn't speak. He types. And types some more. Finally he says, "She's fine. Her heart is good."

"And the bite?" I ask.

"That too," he says. "Let's have the next puppy."

Zoe and I smile at each other and I go out to get Mr. Orange. The process of the examination is repeated, with the exception of the vet's delicate search for testicles. We watch him He looks out the window as his fingers do their work. Finally, he nods and reaches for his stethoscope.

"Well," I ask. "Does he have two?"

"Yes," he says. "There're two."

I let out a long breath and Zoe sighs, this time with relief.

The examination of the heart seems to take a long time, and with each passing second, our anxiety grows. When he finishes, he goes to the computer to type out his official report which I guess is sent to the AKC. Then he speaks. "His heart is okay. His bite is good."

I feel like dancing around the exam table, but I don't.

The other four puppies check out with flying colors and we carry them back to the van. I walk Mattie around the parking area so she can pee while Zoe calls Melanie on the cellphone. I know that Melanie will be on the phone immediately to McKey telling him that he can now call Miss Red Rosalind, and to Rob saying that Mr. Orange is now River Bear Robert's Mr. McKey, named after Zoe's father. He'll be called Mac just like her dad was nicknamed when they moved to Easthampton in 1942.

Chapter Thirteen

A Little Night Music

I'm in bed awake. It must be two o'clock in the morning. The room is dark. My eyes see nothing, but my ears attend to the sounds of the night. Far out on Highway 9 a semi grinds its way up the steep hill out of Pioneer Valley. Slowly the pounding of its pistons fade into the cool night air and silence returns. Out on the lawn a cricket conductor raises his baton and a chorus of crickets strike up their band. Inside, Jamie snores. Her big chest pulls in quantities of air through loose jowls, vibrating them sonorously. She gags as if she's going to cough up something unpleasant, but doesn't. Her snoring stops. She breaths deeply, mellifluously, like the sound of surf on a beach. It's so soothing it could put a person to sleep.

But not me.

In the distance a dog barks. Ellie stands. Did she hear the barking? No, she's just stretching. She shakes her head with the loud flapping of jowls that only Ellie can make. Then she drinks from the bowl of water next to our heat register. Her lapping is smooth, unlike the sound of Bess drinking. Even in the darkness, I can tell when Bess drinks because she bites the water, gulping it down. When Ellie finishes her drink, she shakes her head, dispelling water drops across the room. I feel her chin press down on the end of the bed searching for a spot empty of feet. Finding it she leaps onto the bed, all one hundred and thirty-five pounds of her, and comes up toward us. A black mass rises over me, then lowers itself toward my face. She gives me a kiss from lips still dripping from her drink. Turning around twice, she lies down next to me.

Toenails click across the bare wood floor of the hall. Feet clomp down the stairs. The dog door bangs open. Moments later Bess barks a warning at a suspicious wild scent emanating from the river bank twenty feet below our dog yard fence. Just as I'm ready to get up and go to the window to call Bess in, I hear the dog door bang again. She's inside and crossing through the family room. The puppies smell their mother and wake up. They squeal and bark. One of them says, "Bow, wow, wow," — just like a comic strip dog. I smile. Another goes "Woff, woff." They're growing up. Bess ignores them and climbs the stairs, clomp, clomp, flopping down on the floor at the end of our bed like a bag of cement. The puppies go back to sleep. Silence returns.

Crunch, crunch. Last winter that would have been the rats in the walls until I got rid of them. Now it's Mattie chewing on a banister rail, putting herself to sleep like a baby sucking a pacifier. Patsy clicks her toenails down the hall from the bathroom, her usual place to retire when she's not on Melanie's bed, and jumps up on our bed. Later in the morning when it's time to get up, she'll give us both hugs and kisses, but now she simply curls up next to Zoe.

Outside I hear the mournful, wet warble of a screech owl. The dogs don't hear it. It repeats its call three or four times, then I hear it no more. It must have flown away. A car passes on the road sending its headlights circling around the walls of our bedroom. I hear it every morning about this time. I've decided it's a night nurse coming home from her shift at the hospital, but who knows?

Each place we've lived has had its own night music. In Marblehead, before we moved here, we were lulled to sleep by the sound of surf on the beach and the mournful drone of the foghorn near the harbor entrance. Fifty years ago in Pensacola, Florida, when I was in flight training, it was the roar of the engines as the SNJ Navy training planes took off to make early morning landings on an aircraft carrier, a sound that sent chills down my spine. I knew my time was coming to make those landings, and, with Melanie just born, I dreaded it. I eventually dropped out and was sent to Japan. There the night music was more pleasant: the click of *geta* as our late-night Japanese neighbors came home on the lane outside our bedroom window. In the early, still dark mornings it was the squeak of the tofu salesman's bicycle and the tune he played on his pipe. When we were students at the University of Chicago it was the woman with five children from the next door basement apartment scratching on our door telling us she was dying. She died almost every night. When I was a child in Flint, Michigan, it was the slow, labored chug, chug, chug of locomotives straining under heavy loads of Fischer Body car chassis. As the engine struggled, suddenly the drive wheels would slip and the steam engine would emit a rapid chugchugchug. Then it would start all over again with a slow chug, chug, chug.

Zoe moans in her sleep and Jamie wakes up to see if she's all right. I touch her shoulder and rub it gently. She relaxes. Patsy and Ellie shift their positions, squeezing more closely against us. It's comforting.

When I was about ten I had a dog that slept with me. I got him as a puppy. Named him Chris. He was half Dalmatian and half pointer and had a bobbed tail like our current puppy, Mr. White. When he was little we tied him to a leg of the stove in the kitchen, but as soon as he was housebroken, he slept with me. We didn't neuter dogs then, nor were we required to keep them tied up or fenced. When Chris wanted to go out we opened the door and out he went. Twice he got lost and my sister drove me up and down the streets of Flint, looking for him. I hung out the window calling, "Chris! Here Chris!" Two or three days later we found him tired and hungry. Another time when we couldn't find him after a long search we called the dog pound. "Yeah, we got 'em." When we went to get him, he had a broken leg. The attendant said, "The story we heard is he got rejected by his girlfriend and he jumped off the bridge into the Flint River. They found him down on the river bank." The leg was set in a cast on which Chris became so proficient he could even run. I had Chris through high school until I went away to the University of Michigan. One day Mom called me to say that Chris had died. She was crying. I cried, too. What a friend that dog had been.

Thinking of Mom, my ambling thoughts move on to Dad who never was that fond of Chris. A dog's place was outside, not in the house. Dad grew up on a farm north of Flint. Farmers, generally, kept their dogs outside. Dad came into town to attend high school. He lived with an aunt and gave up his farmer ways.

After graduation he got a job as teller in a local bank, and worked himself up to a fairly successful position. I'm told that at one time we even had two Buicks. My brother and two sisters were eleven, nine and seven years older than I, so, as a baby, I was idolized and loved much like a puppy. Seven months after I was born, my family's world of limitless opportunity ended with the 1929 market crash. Dad crashed too and never really regained his self-esteem. The man I knew as my father was a furniture salesman who worked for other people who, unlike my father, appeared to sail gracefully through the Depression. Bitter but kind, he considered himself a failure and not entitled to overt anger. Once when I was about sixteen, I returned from a camping trip and was putting our car into the garage. I'd left the right rear door open, a door that was hinged toward the rear of car. I took out the center post of our two car garage and almost ripped the door off the car. Dad came out of the house, looked at it and shook his head. "Be more careful next time," was all he said.

A few years ago, long after Dad died, my brother gave me a faded photograph of Dad taken on the farm when he was about fifteen. He's holding the leads of two enormous, strident workhorses and smiling broadly. I wish I could have known this confident, happy young man.

My thoughts drift on through sleeplessness. Since Mac, the former Mr. Orange, will be living with us, I will have to enlarge the outdoor pen we're using to feed the puppies. He will have to be contained when one of our ladies is in heat. In the darkness the project looms larger and larger. Suddenly it becomes imperative that a solution be found right there in my bed in the middle of the night. I plan how I'll extend the left side over to the wall of the house, and move the gate to the other side facing the river. Then I can get the snow blower into the pen to remove the snow that slides off the shed roof. I go around and around with this idea, until I realize that I won't be able to get into the pen from the dog yard to feed the puppies. So how can I construct the fence to . . .

Fortunately Ellie unlocks me from this repetitive circumambulation of the fence problem by getting up, turning around and putting her head on my pillow next to mine. She gives me a single kiss, then goes back to sleep. Jamie, on the floor beside Zoe, does her part by licking herself with a lap, lap, lap, lap as annoying as a dripping faucet. Just when I can stand no more, she stops. At least, I forget the fence issue.

When I was still working at the Massachusetts Port Authority I would wake up at this time of night in our little condo in the Bay Village section of Boston. Sometimes the giggles of a prostitute servicing a John in the alley below our window would awaken me. But more often it was worry over something going on at the office. How was I going to justify to the Board a promotional expense which was beyond budget? How could I bring one of our foreign consultants into line when he'd already convinced my boss to accept a preposterous marketing scheme? I would lie awake terrified that I was going to be fired, or furious at being manipulated. These problems which loomed large in night's darkness generally regained perspective with the light of dawn, but at night they kept me awake.

Now I'm retired. All that's in the past. I'm awake in the middle of the night and, for the most part, am enjoying it. I reach down and pull up another blanket. The nights are getting cold, even with two dogs and Zoe to keep me warm. Tomorrow, or rather later today when the sun comes up, it'll be Sunday morning. I think I'll go to church. Lately, with all the puppy duties in the morning, I've skipped church. The truth is, I preferred to stay at home with Zoe. Sometimes I ask myself, how much longer will Zoe and I have together? How much longer do I have to enjoy the companionship and love I cherish more than anything else in life? But It doesn't mean I have to be with Zoe every minute. She can be busy with her things, and I with mine. Like the way we are right now. She's asleep and I'm awake, but I can reach out and touch her shoulder to make sure she's there. Still, I think I'll go to church. I miss my friends there and maybe Penny Schultz, our music director, will be rehearsing the choir. I love to sing.

That will be later this morning after we've fed the puppies and the dogs, cleaned up the puppy poop from the X-pen and the dog yard, had breakfast and vacuumed the downstairs.

For now, I listen to the river singing joyously from the rain of tropical storm Francis. My hand reaches over to Zoe and comes to rest on the curve of her back. My eyes grows heavy. Gradually I fall . . .

Chapter Fourteen

Goodbye Mr. White

"I'm not selling any of the puppies," Zoe says as the little ones gather around her chair in the grassy play yard. It's Sunday afternoon and we're sitting in the cool shade of the barn. Miss Purple has seized Zoe's newspaper and is pulling it from her lap. Ros is trying to knock over her cup of tea that sits on a small plastic table. The other puppies are under the steps that come down to the play yard from the dog yard. This is the second day the puppies have come down the steps by themselves. Mr. White sticks his head, haloed in thick black fur, through the opening between the steps. Floppy ears, like two big pancakes, frame his face. The tip of his tongue is just visible. He looks at us with black shiny eyes which seem to say, "I can see you, but you can't see me." Something sparks Mr. Blue's interest and he dashes out from under the steps. A fleet of puppies follow, waving their tails in the air like semaphore flags signaling their happiness. Suddenly their frantic, tumbling race along the stone wall toward the river comes to a stop. They concentrate on some new found mystery in a clump of weeds.

"No," Zoe says, "I'm keeping all six of them."

The other day when the cardiologist passed all six hearts, we hadn't even arrived home before someone called saying they wanted to buy Mr. White. This was good news because it is Mr. White's tail that had to be bobbed. They want a male Newfoundland for a pet and don't mind if his tail is a little short. They had called Betty McDonnell asking if she knew of any breeders having puppies, and Betty referred them to Zoe. They'll be here in a few minutes.

While I was at church, Zoe and Melanie gave Mr. White a bath, dried him with the blow-dryer until he was a ball of fur, and trimmed his toenails. Earlier Zoe made a folder containing Mr. White's pedigree, tracing it back through several generations, his medical records, what he's eating and the amounts, and several useful suggestions for the new owner. On the cover of the folder she put an 8 x 10 picture of Mr. White that Melanie had taken the day before. Everything is ready. Everything, but not everyone.

"I'm not selling Mr. White," Zoe asserts.

A car pulls into the driveway. "They're here," I say. Zoe exhales a long, deep breath of resignation and gets up.

We go up to the house and bring the adopting parents in through the front door. It's always a problem bringing people into our house. We want to get them inside before they meet the ladies, and we don't want the ladies to get out the front door. Fortunately, old houses have doors on every room so the door to the family room is closed with the dogs on the other side.

We meet Dave and Veronica, an attractive young couple who are obviously excited about getting a puppy. Once inside with the outside door closed, we open the door to the family room and our five ladies surge into the narrow entrance hall to meet Mr. White's new owners.

"My goodness!" Veronica says, "they *are* big." Ellie, who weighs much more than Veronica and would be taller than she if she stood on her hind feet, is nudging our guest back against the newel post. For a minute I'm afraid Veronica will change her mind about Newfoundlands. "Is this one a male?" she asks.

With one of my usual absent-minded responses, I reply, "Oh no, this is Ellie. Males are much bigger." Veronica gives me an enigmatic frown the uncertain meaning of which scares me. Maybe they'll change their mind about a male Newfoundland puppy.

Dave is reserved, and seems to handle with ease the sniffing noses and pressing black shoulders. We move into the family room where the melee is joined by six puppies running in and out of the big dogs' legs.

"Oh my," Veronica says, "They're adorable. Which one is Mr. White?"

The colored yarns we tied on the puppies to tell them apart when they were little has long since been replaced with collars. We couldn't find a white collar, so Mr. White is wearing one that is red and white. But there's no doubt about which is Mr. White. His shorter tail is wagging rapidly as he scurries to the fore. "I'm right here," he seems to say.

Zoe picks him up and hands him to Veronica. Mr. White is now a twenty-four pound bundle of twisting body and pumping legs. Just as he's about to fly from Veronica's arms, Dave catches him and cuddles him against his chest. Mr. White looks up at him, then snuggles his head against Dave's shoulder. Dave looks at us and smiles. Veronica gives Mr. White a kiss. It's a match.

Zoe shows them the folder she's made for Mr. White and for half an hour discusses dog food, crates for the nighttime, house breaking, exercise, training and, most important, Newfoundland owner contacts. Dave and Veronica live in the region of New York State served by the Bear Mountain Newfoundland Club. Here they will find Newfoundland breeders and pet owners who can answer their questions about veterinarians, puppy kindergartens, dog obedience trainers and club activities such as Newfoundland Fun Days.

Zoe had asked them to bring pictures of their house and yard so we could be sure Mr. White is going to a good home with a large fenced yard. Veronica runs to the car and returns with a photo album two inches thick. She's proud of her house.

"Here it is before we started the renovation. Dave's a finished carpenter so he did all of the work himself. You can see the yard. Here there's no fence." She turns some pages. "And here's the house after we've fixed it up and the yard with its stockade fence. It's one hundred by sixty feet."

"That should do it," I say. "Just make sure he doesn't dig underneath. Mattie, here, is a digger. She has an escape tunnel she's working on under the dog yard fence."

It's time for them to go. No use prolonging it. Zoe picks up Mr. White and carries him to the car. Veronica opens the trunk from which she extracts all manner of puppy paraphernalia: a comfy little bed with padded sides that's way too small for Mr. White, chewy toys that he'll love and a jug of water in case he gets thirsty.

Zoe is still holding Mr. White. Her eyes

are getting misty. It's hard to let go of those you love.

One day back in 1970 Zoe and I were sitting on the top deck of our boat in an inlet to the Rappahannock River in Virginia. We'd sneaked out of the rectory and away from the parish for a night alone. Daniel and I had rebuilt an old oyster boat so that it looked like a tugboat with a pilot house and a cabin. We were sitting on the deck above the cabin, drinking martinis, feeling like we were on a honeymoon away from our kids and parishioners when we heard our little aluminum motorboat churning up the inlet. It was our son Daniel. He'd found us.

"I just don't want to go to William and Mary," he said for openers. This, of course, couldn't have waited until we returned the next morning.

"But you need the student deferment," I explained. "You've got a low number." It was the Vietnam War we were concerned about.

"I know," he said. "That's why I want to enlist in the Coast Guard." Hurrying on so we'd have no time to argue, he said, "I've found out I can go to boot camp and then apply to the academy." He was remembering that I had been an officer in the Navy. I'd told him often that being an officer was an easier life than being enlisted.

We said we'd think about it and see him in the morning. I've always admired the Coast Guard and, with the mess we were in in Vietnam, it sounded like a good way to fulfill his service obligation. Zoe seemed to agree and the next day we told him we had no objections.

When it was time for him to go, the whole family drove him to Richmond to catch a bus with the other recruits. His sisters, Melanie and Martha, were sad to see him go and Zoe was close to tears. Daniel, looking far younger than his eighteen years, was scared. I'm enthusiastic because I'm remembering the comradeship I had with the other men at Officer Candidate School. What I was forgetting was that I was six years older than Daniel is now. Hiding tears, he hugged his mom and boarded the bus.

His time in the Coast Guard was a series of disappointments. Fortunately, while stationed in Norfolk, he found friends who were followers of Maher Baba, the avatar, who eventually led him to Carolyn, the person who would become his wife.

Two years after Daniel left, I gave Melanie away to her husband in a wedding ceremony to end all wedding ceremonies. Organ, timpani and trumpet provided the music, and colorful banners preceded the bride down the aisle. At the reception on the banks of the Rappahannock River, we all waved to the newlyweds as they departed on their honeymoon aboard a small yacht. Nineteen years later, Melanie, sick with Hepatitis C and divorced from her husband, is back with us. But her strong spirit and determination turned a disastrous marriage into a chance for her boys to excel in their chosen fields of art and the theater.

Martha, our youngest, left us three times. First, for a full scholarship at Tufts University where she stayed for only one semester. She returned home for two years at the community college, then left for the University of Virginia to complete her BA degree. The third leaving was for New York and a job with the Oxford University Press as a copy writer. New York terrified me when we'd go to visit her. I was afraid to leave the car on the street and to leave Martha at her apartment on 89th Street near Amsterdam. But Martha soon became friends with the shopkeepers and the other apartment dwellers nearby, and made a home for herself in New York.

Wanting but not wanting to let them go, we knew we must because it was time. How much we felt that way last year when it was time to let our old beloved Bear leave us.

He would try to get up to go outside to poop, but he couldn't get his back legs under him. I'd slip a towel under his belly and, holding the ends, pull up his rear. Walking with him, being his back legs, we'd go to the dog yard. He'd do his business, then stand there on wobbly legs and look at me. He was embarrassed. It's hard when an old gentleman can no longer take care of his basic needs. And he was probably in pain, although he never cried out.

"It's time," I said to Zoe.

"No," she replied. "Not just yet. I want to take him swimming one last time."

I tried to visualize taking him down the stone steps to the river. "We'd never make it. He's too heavy to carry."

"Melanie says there's a place downriver where we can park the car next to the bank."

We lifted Bear into the back of the Subaru, because it's lower than the van, and found the place Melanie was talking about. The path to the river was about thirty feet and not too steep. The spot was beautiful with overhanging trees and a sandy river bank. Holding Bear's backend in the towel, I helped him down the path. He saw, heard and smelled the river, and I could hardly walk fast enough to keep up with him.

Zoe hooked a long leash to his collar and together we waded with him into the water. Soon he reached a spot where he could float with just the tips of his feet touching bottom. Standing upright, his backend supported by the water, he walked out a little farther, turned around and looked at us. It was like old times in Marblehead when he used to hang out in the deep water not wanting to come in. He looked up at a bird sitting on a branch above him, until it flew away. Then he turned his head upriver where the water cascaded over a rock ledge. In spite of his dead pan expression, we knew he was enjoying it. Finally he grew tired and came back to us.

That night Zoe made a bed for herself on the floor of the family room next to Bear. With his head in her arms, they fell asleep.

The next day we went to the vet's. We'd made a bed for Bear in back of the van right behind the front seats so Zoe could pet him all the way there. The vet came out to the van to perform his grim task. With Bear's head in Zoe's lap, the vet gave our old friend a shot. Bear flinched, but only once, then returned his head to Zoe's lap. He relaxed and soon he was gone.

When we got home I drove across the orchard to a grave McKey had dug above the river. Wrapping Bear in his favorite sheepskin blanket, McKey and I lifted him into the grave. With tears and sobbing all around we said our goodbyes to Bear, recalling the good times we'd had together, his deadpan expression that hid his sense of humor and the joy we'd known in the many years we'd had together.

Zoe hands Mr. White to Dave. "What are you going to name him?" she asks.

"Oscar," Veronica says from the seat.

"That's a good name," Zoe says, forcing a smile.

Dave hands Oscar to Veronica who, I think, has this idea that young Oscar will curl up in her lap. Not at all. He wants to shift the gearshift, turn the steering wheel, explore the floor and climb onto the dashboard. Dave runs to the driver's side and gets in. Doors are shut. We wave last farewells, and off they go.

"Goodbye, Oscar," we cry.

Chapter Fifteen

Eleanor Roosevelt
Slept Here

*L*ocal legend has it that Eleanor Roosevelt slept in our house, probably in our very own bedroom. The story is that she came to West Cummington in 1933 or '34 as part of a program to revitalize community pride during the dark days of the Depression. The idea was to remind the local citizenry of past achievements by changing, at least for the day, the name of the town to reflect past industry. The name chosen for West Cummington was Paper Mill Village.

I can see it now. On the dirt road in front of our house Mrs. Roosevelt is standing on a hastily constructed wooden platform decorated with colorful bunting. A couple of horse drawn wagons and a line of Model A cars are parked nearby. The school band is playing a rousing march. Members of the Board of Selectmen are standing behind her. A sullen crowd wanting jobs, not platitudes mingles in front of the stand. The music concludes and the First Lady begins. She reminds them of the paper mill that stood across the road a generation earlier. How it employed eighty workers and supported a population of 400 people here in West Cummington. The paper it produced was of the finest quality and was shipped around the world. Then, in my fantasy, she outlines her husband's efforts to restore employment through the WPA, the CCC and the NRA. She tells them that money has been appropriated for a CCC project that will hire unemployed men and women right here in West Cummington for the building of roads and parks. At the prospects for work, the crowd cheers, and she ends on a high note.

Then she crosses the road, enters our house, has dinner with the Goodnow family who were the owners at that time, and settles down for the night in our bedroom.

Whatever happened on her visit to West Cummington, Zoe is inspired to name our second dog after the lady with whom we share our bedroom, a lady whom Zoe and I both admire. Like Eleanor Roosevelt, Ellie takes on the role of concerned leader, looking out for the underdog, and seeing that justice is done.

When Ellie came to our house as a puppy it was an event Bear hadn't had since Clara arrived five years earlier. At nine years old, Bear could still run and play, and immediately Ellie became his playmate. Down by the river he would chase little Ellie along the sandy bank and around the trees until Ellie escaped into a rock crevice in an old stone wall. She'd yap at Bear who pawed the earth and barked at the coal black eyes and bundle of fur hidden far back in the rock hole. "Come out of there you little pup," Bear would bark.

"Not on your life, big boy," she'd retort.

The rock wall was part of what's left of a stone and wooden dam that crossed the river behind our house. The dam and the mile long millpond it created provided the power for the paper mill across the road. A flume, still buried somewhere under the dogs' play yard, carried the water beneath our property and beneath the road to the mill. Now the ancient rocks provided a sanctuary for Ellie from which she could tease Bear with puppy bravado.

Ellie has grown into a very large and lovely Newfoundland. She has one major and four points toward a championship, but has lost interest in pursuing the title. Instead, working with Zoe, she received her CD (Companion Dog) title for obedience and qualified as a therapy dog. How fitting for her gentle temperament. Zoe takes her to our daughter Martha's seventh grade class where the children take turns petting her during reading time. I built a cart for Ellie to pull, and Zoe is training her in carting. Last Christmas, Ellie, bedecked with sleigh bells, pulled the cart filled with Christmas cookies to the homes of our neighbors. With her was our family and Martha's, including some friends, dressed in Harry Potter capes which Melanie had made. Two of the grandchildren led the procession carrying touches. Our neighbors were astonished, to say the least, when they came to the door. Ellie didn't drop a single cookie.

It's a strange day. The one-time hurricane, Ivan the Terrible, now a tropical storm, is dumping several inches of rain over the Hampshire Hills. The thousands of little streams that run down from the hills have swollen into torrents all feeding the Westfield River. I walk through the rain down to the play yard and over to the gate leading down to the river. As I ponder the rushing waters, Ellie appears behind me at the top of the steps to the play yard. She's concerned about my standing in the rain and calls to me with her worried bark/howl, "Woowoowoowoo." I invite her to come down and join me. She doesn't much like the idea of being out in the rain, but she comes down to the gate and presses her big head against my leg. I rub her ear.

We don't go down to the river. It would be too dangerous. The sandy beach where she played as a puppy is under two feet of water that reaches almost to the rocks in which she hid from Bear. Pale brown, foam-crested water is roaring over the rock ledge that stretches out into the river from our shore. Not a bit of the three foot ledge is visible. An enormous tree with broken branches like the spines of a fantasy dragon has ridden the deluge over the ledge and into our once quiet pool where it has wedged itself against our bank. I'm mesmerized by the ominous, surging power of the river and cannot move.

I wonder what thoughts pass through Ellie's mind as she watches this spectacle of nature's power. Are there memories of the times she played on its banks with Bear? Are premonitions of a fearful future aroused by the flooding waters? More likely she is wondering why I'm standing here and hoping I will soon return to the house. Not so with me. There's something foreboding about the water's violence that holds me here as if it has a message about the future I can't quite read.

Ellie shakes the rain from her coat and seems to say, "Enough of this brooding. Let's get out of the rain and go inside." Or am I putting words into her WooWooWoo? We turn back to the house.

Saturday morning I make the weekly trip to the recycling center, a.k.a. The Dump, with garbage, can/plastic/glass and newspapers for recycling, and empty soda cans for the men at the center to redeem. In the van I also have the family room sofa which must weigh a couple hundred pounds. One of the men at the center helps me lift it out of the van and into the huge dumpster.

"What happened to the sofa?" Mike asks. He's looking at the ripped upholstery, chewed arm rests and exposed stuffing.

"The dogs ate it," I say.

"How do you stop them from doing that?"

"We don't. We just get another sofa from the Salvation Army Resale."

And that's what Melanie and Zoe had done the day before. Getting the old one out of the house and into the van through the pouring rain, and the replacement into the family room, was more exhausting than I had realized. We achieved it, thanks to Martha's help when she came by to deliver an apple pie from her church bakesale. Hence my not feeling well today — from the exertion, not the pie. When I overdo it, the arthritis in my neck tightens up giving me headaches and I feel like a have a Newfoundland lying on my chest when I breath.

Returning from the dump, I feel light headed, so I go to the bedroom and lie down. This is the second time today I've lain down, and the comfortable bed feels so good it's scary.

Ellie senses that I'm not feeling well. She comes into the bedroom, looks at me, then jumps onto the bed and licks my face. It's not one lick, it's a face wash. After a very wet minute she decides her medicinal ablutions are sufficient to cure what ails me, and lies down beside me. I dry my face on the sheet and pat her shoulder, still wet from the rain.

Ellie is consistently thoughtful. Each morning after she has managed to convince us that it's time to get up and feed the pack, the whole crew follows Zoe to the head of the stairs. Zoe takes one step downward and all the dogs except Ellie charge down the stairs with much barking. Ellie waits for Zoe to arrive safely at the bottom, then comes down.

Ellie was a wonderful mother the one time she gave birth to a litter of three puppies. She stepped around them in the whelping box with the grace of a ballerina. When her little babies curled out their tiny poops, Ellie cleaned them up immediately. Even now, when her daughter Patsy was in heat, she was so persistent in cleaning up her discharge that it was hard for Zoe to get a sample.

In the play yard, when Mathilda's and Bess's play-fighting gets a bit too rough, Ellie will charge into the fray and tell them to cool it. They pretty much ignore her, but she seems to feel better. Now that Bess's puppies are romping about the house, they love to tease Ellie. Mac will come up to her when she lying on the sofa and try to kiss her. Ellie will rumble a quiet growl that seems to say, "I'm not your mother kid. Go away." Mac sits down with his face about six inches from Ellie's nose and barks.

The mattress begins to absorb my neck pains, and lying down doesn't require me to force much air into my pressured lungs. I tell myself it will pass. It's only a little cold combined with arthritis combined with overexertion. I do this about every three months. In another three days my grandson, William, is coming over and we'll finish the expansion of the fence to enclose Mac when the ladies are in heat. By then I'll feel my old self again, I tell myself. But I'm having trouble believing it. When you're feeling down, it seems like it'll last forever.

"They're here," Melanie calls from downstairs. Bess barks, Mathilda and Patsy join her, and Ellie leaps from the bed. The people from Rochester have arrived to take Miss Purple.

By the time I get downstairs, Zoe and Melanie have shut the dogs in the family room and are standing at the front door welcoming

Miss Purple's new family. A young mother and father with three excited daughters are coming up the steps. We usher them into the living room, then cautiously open the family room door. The Westfield River surging with the power of the storm, Ivan, can't compare with the onslaught of five adult Newfoundlands eager to greet guests.

Fortunately, the family has had Newfoundlands so they have some idea what to expect. The two older daughters, six and eight, dance and giggle when the dogs wrap them in black fur and give them kisses, but the youngest one, age three, is rescued by her father and held in his arms for the remainder of their stay. We take them down to the play yard followed by the dogs and the puppies. The rain has ended and the sun has come out. The puppies fall in love with the two older girls and chase them around the yard. The father finds Miss Purple and asks about the out-of-joint tail.

"Does it cause her any trouble?"

"No," I answer. "She just wags a little more to the right than the left." We've all fallen desperately in love with Miss Purple and we want to find her a good home where they'll raise her as a pet. He touches the one bone at the base of the tail that's slightly out of joint.

"It's hardly noticeable," he says. "We

don't plan to show her anyway." He tells me they have a large fenced yard right on the shore of Lake Ontario. "We're going to train her for water work."

"She should be good at that," I say. "Her mom, Bess, loves the water."

Zoe and his wife finish the paper work for the transfer of Miss Purple to her new family and we gather around their car. A sturdy crate with a soft quilt in it is strapped to the floor behind the front seat. The three girls are seated behind it. They are so excited they can't stop giggling.

Zoe is holding Miss Purple who is cuddling into her arms. Melanie gives the puppy a kiss, then I kiss her. I can see that Zoe doesn't want to let her go. When we took newborn Purple to the vet, he told Zoe that the only way to straighten the tail was surgery, and even that was doubtful. Zoe didn't want to put her through that. Instead, she raised her with an abundance of love and watchful care. She hands Miss Purple to the husband, wishes them well, and with tears shining in the corners of her eyes, hurries to the house. It makes no difference that these are the perfect owners for Miss Purple. We know they will love and protect her and raise her to be a good pet and probably an expert water dog. It's just so darn hard to let go of a puppy you love like one of your own family.

Why do we put ourselves in this spot? Why do we take them into our home and lavish them with love, only to go through the heartbreak of having them leave? I guess it's because the sadness of letting them go is fractional compared to the great joy of having them for twelve weeks.

I follow Zoe to the house, take her in my arms, and we both cry.

Chapter Sixteen

Laughter

It's five in the morning, and still dark as night. The puppies are barking up a storm. They've spent their first night in the outdoor pen and they want the world to know it's not as nice as the X-pen in the dining room. Actually they can go from the pen through a dog door into a kennel in the shed if they want to be inside, but maybe they haven't figured that out yet. Bess goes down to see what's going on and exchanges barks with her puppies.

"I'm getting up," Zoe says. "I can't stand it. I've got to see if they're all right." She puts on her bathrobe against the chilly morning and goes down. Letting them out of the pen, she crosses the dog yard to the back door while they tug at her robe.

"What do you mean leaving us outside all night?" their barks complain. "We're supposed to sleep in the dining room."

I make coffee, and Zoe and I manage another few minutes in bed reading and waking up.

At six o'clock I hear puppies climbing the stairs. Peeking into the the hall I see that Mac is half way up the stairs. The other three puppies are down below at the bottom.

"Come on guys," I interpret him saying. "Don't be afraid."

Ros cautiously climbs three steps and stops. Mr. Blue and Miss Green come to step number two. Ros calls up to Mac. "It's so high up there. What if we fall?"

"Aw Ros, you can make it. See, I'm going all the way to the top."

Ros comes up another three steps. Blue and Green follow. Green says, "Sorry friends, I'm going back down." Turning around on the step, she almost knocks Blue over.

"Take it easy, Green. I'm not a monkey."

"Naw," Mac calls down. "You're a chicken."

"Am not," Blue shouts, and climbs to within two steps of the top.

"Wait for me," Ros barks, and bunny hops up the steps. Green follows. Now three puppies are crammed onto two steps near the top.

As I watch, I begin to laugh. Zoe calls to me from the bedroom. "What's happening?"

"Come see."

She comes into the hall and, looking at the puppies on the stairs, her smiles turn to laughter. Mac sees her and runs over, then immediately back again to the top of the stairs.

"Hurry up, you guys," he encourages. "There's another whole house up here." They've already turned around and are tumbling down the stairs. The big dogs have gathered at the bottom.

"Were we ever as cute as my puppies?" Mother Bess seems to say.

"Were we ever that nuts?" Grandmother Jamie adds.

The three puppies no sooner hit bottom than they turn around and head back up. This time they make the peak of the mountain. "We made it," Ros proclaims, "and we're still alive."

"Let's do it again," Blue says. It's not the victory of gaining the peak, it's the fun of climbing. Down all four of them go, bounce off the bottom step and run back up.

Zoe and I can't stop laughing.

Mac says, "Wanna see the bathroom? There's a big tub. You can look inside." The three follow Mac into the bathroom, snatching a quick drink from the big dogs' water bowl, and look at the bathtub. Then out, down the hall and into our bedroom. Green grabs the edge of a quilt and starts to pull it off the bed. Blue has my dirty socks from yesterday. Ros has been lifted onto the bed by Zoe and, finding her coffee cup, spills it onto the bedside table. Mac is checking out the study and all the fascinating computer wires behind the desk.

"Time to get up." I say. As I go down the stairs, I call, "Pup, pup, pup, pup. Time for poops and pees." They tumble down the stairs behind me and we head for the dining room door. Blue stops midway to pee in the family room. I sigh, "He was that close."

When Zoe has prepared their breakfast pans, I carry them to the pen, followed by the puppies. I lower the pans through a mass of swirling black bodies and gnashing teeth. There's plenty for everybody, but Mac tries to secure a whole pan for himself with a macho growl. Mr. Blue ignores him and helps himself to the food in the pan.

I shake my head and laugh. What other life could provide so much laughter? We could use our limited funds to travel, but we've done that. Or we could have toys like new cars or a camper. Or go to the theater or a Celtic basketball game whenever we wanted. But nothing I can think of comes close to the fun of having puppies. I see ads on TV for retirement communities where a man and woman are carrying their golf bags onto a manicured course. I wish them well, but how often will they laugh?

The arthritis that seized my neck, and the general malaise I felt two days ago have eased somewhat. I'm seeing our doctor in a couple of days and I know she'll say, "Well Dan, you're not as young as you used to be." And I'll answer,

"That's why we have puppies."

Zoe has an agreement with a couple to purchase Mr. Blue. They arrive after a five and half hour drive and are very personable and anxious to buy a puppy.

I take them down to the play yard where there is sufficient space for them to meet the big dogs and see the puppies. The wife asks to hold Mr. Blue and Zoe brings him to her. As the rest of us talk, she does her best to cuddle him. But Mr. Blue squirms away and lies down ten feet from her, eying her suspiciously.

"Is he sick?" she asks. "He doesn't seem to have any life. Has he always been that independent?"

Zoe is alarmed. Mr. Blue seemed just fine all morning. It's clear, however, that he's acting very strange.

They ask if they can spend some time with him alone, so we go into the house with the other dogs. About ten minutes later, they come in holding Blue, and say, "We decided that he isn't the dog for us. We're looking for a puppy that's less independent and more cuddly."

Financially this is a blow to us, because we'd taken Blue off the market for a whole week. But Zoe says, "Well, since that's the way you feel, it's best you don't take him."

I try to say something nice. "I guess there just isn't a match."

So they leave, and Mr. Blue remains with us. Immediately we check him over. His nose is moist. He seems alert. When we put him down he runs to the other puppies and chews Ros's ear. Mr. Blue is in fine shape. So what happened?

He didn't like them. He didn't want to go with them and he wasn't going to have anything to do with them.

How about that? If they had taken him, Mr. Blue would have been miserable and so would his new owners. And we would have been desolate. Blue knew what was best.

Our hope was to have all the puppies sold, except for Mac and Ros, before Patsy whelps. The thought of having four twelve week-old puppies to take care of at the same time we're dealing with newborn pups seemed like a lot of work. But it looks like that's the way it'll be. Today Melanie takes Patsy to the vet for X-rays, and we'll find out just how many puppies she has.

With only six days left until Patsy is scheduled to whelp, and keeping in mind that Bess was two days early, I set up the whelping box in the living room. As I'm working, I think of the days ahead. For three weeks Zoe,

Melanie and I will be standing watches twenty-four hours a day. I remember the midnight feedings, the struggle to stay awake, and the constant fear that the mother might step on a puppy. And I remember going shopping during the day and standing in the plastic wraps aisle unable to wake up enough to find a food storage bag with twist ties.

Then Mac and Ros bound into the living room where I'm kneeling on the floor removing a large roll of plastic from a box. They climb on my arms and try to bite my chin. "Thanks, but no thanks," I say. "I don't need your help." I'm about to cut a six foot section of plastic to put under the whelping box. Laying down the heavy roll of plastic on the floor, I go the kitchen to get scissors. When I come back they have unrolled about twenty feet and are piercing the plastic with tiny teeth holes. They look at me as if I should thank them for their efforts. I laugh and hug them both.

Melanie calls home on the cellphone as soon as she comes out of the vet's office. "Patsy is fine and has at least three puppies. Maybe four."

It's late evening. Melanie is still downstairs with the puppies who have not yet been put to bed in the outdoor pen. Zoe and I are in bed reading. The phone rings, Melanie answers it and calls up to Zoe. "It's for you, Mom."

It's Melanie Peck. She and her husband, Ted, own the Newf Emporium that specializes in clothing, art work, books and other paraphernalia pertaining to Newfoundlands. We met them four years ago at a Newfoundland dog show where they had a concession stand. Since then we've become friends and they are selling some of Grandson Rob's prints of Newfoundlands.

"Hi Zoe, it's Melanie Peck. Do you have any puppies left?"

'Yes, we do. A male and a female. Are you interested?"

"We are and we'd like to come there on Saturday to buy one of them."

And so it goes. In less than twenty-four hours, the picture has changed again. Now we'll have only one extra puppy to think about when Patsy whelps.

So as not to be caught unprepared for the whelping, Zoe and Melanie transform the living room into a whelping dispensary. Shelves are cleared of books and knickknacks, and replaced with baby bottles, two syringes, hypodermic needles, iodine, Vaseline, thermometer, dental floss (for tying umbilical cords), sterile pads, cotton balls, etc. The baby scale is on a shelf ready to record birth weights and daily growth. Several strands of colored yarn are lined up to tie onto the newborns' necks for identification.

Saturday afternoon Ted and Melanie arrive dressed for the luncheon they've attended earlier that day. "Mind if we change into jeans before we greet the dogs?" Melanie asks. She knows Newfoundlands. They have two. When they're ready we introduce the five dogs and four puppies, all of which are delighted with the smell of other Newfoundlands on the Pecks' clothes.

In the play yard they begin the process of selecting either Mr. Blue or Miss Green. They can't decide. They've fallen for both. Finally we all come up to the house, dogs included, and Ted and Melanie take the two puppies into the dog yard. They're out there for several minutes while we wait expectantly to hear which puppy they'll take. When they come in, Ted says, "I called each puppy to come to me. Miss Green ran right over, gave me a kiss, then went off to play. Mr. Blue came when I called, gave me a kiss and stayed to play with me. Melanie agrees. We'll take Mr. Blue."

What they don't know is that Mr. Blue chose them. Unlike the last suitors whom he rejected, he could tell that the Pecks would be the perfect owners for him.

"Tell them the name we've decided on," Melanie says to her husband.

"It's my middle name, Wendell. Do you like it?"

"That's perfect," Zoe says.

Our parting with Wendell is made somewhat easier because we know the Pecks as friends. Still, Zoe kisses him good bye at the door and stays inside while I walk the Pecks and Wendell to their car. It's never easy.

Sunday evening arrives and Zoe takes Patsy's temperature. It's still hovering around 100 with no sudden drops. The only time it had gone down was on Friday, but that was only to 99.6, which didn't seem low enough to be significant. Melanie has Patsy sleep in her room with the door closed so she can go out to the dog yard with her during the night. Monday morning comes and while I'm making coffee, I hear Melanie bringing Patsy down. Mel has the towel and the flashlight since it's still dark out. Minutes later they come back in. Not the slightest interest on Patsy's part to drop a pup. It looks like maybe one more day.

Later that morning, and Zoe's worried about Patsy. Something isn't right about the temperature and the position of the pups in the abdomen. If that temperature drop to 99.6 on Friday was significant, then whelping should have taken place in twelve to eighteen hours. We can't afford to take chances. Maybe Patsy's late.

When Jamie's two puppies were born dead two years before, it was about three days after they were due. What we should have done was have a C-section before it was too late.

With this vividly in Zoe's mind, she calls the vet's office as soon as they open. All the staff in the office know our dogs, and if Zoe calls with a problem or question they do all they can to accommodate her. Our regular vet isn't in on Mondays, but they put in a call to him. He'll meet them at his office.

I have to make a quick trip to Pittsfield for some essentials before the puppies are born, so I'm not there when the vet calls back. I'm just starting home when the cellphone rings. It's Zoe.

"He's going to do a C-section and we'll leave just as soon as you can get home."

"I'll be there in half an hour." We live twenty miles from shopping and fifty miles from the vet.

As I pull into the driveway, they're putting Patsy in the van. I wish her good luck and wave as they drive away.

Three anxious hours later, Melanie calls. "He did the C-section. Two males and a female. Patsy's fine now, but there was hemorrhaging in her uterus. It's lucky we took her in. We're on our way home."

Zoe was right. She saw the signs and read them correctly. Thanks to her and our good vet, Patsy and the puppies are alive. I breath a deep sigh of relief.

When they arrive, Melanie leads a still sedated Patsy into the house. I'm sure she has no idea what happened to her, nor the identity of the three small black creatures that I'm carrying into the house in a box.

Zoe's almost in tears. "The poor things were crying all the way home. They're starving."

We settle the babies in a box beneath a lamp to keep them warm and wait for Patsy to come around enough to feed her babies. It's decided that Melanie will take the first watch until midnight and then Zoe the rest of the night. I'll take over when I get up at five.

Tuesday morning when I awake it's pouring rain. I relieve Zoe and take the older puppies outside, then feed them. Next the big dogs are fed and I go to the living room with Patsy in tow. "Come on big girl. Time to feed your babies." While we were feeding Patsy, her babies remained in the cardboard box kept warm with a heating pad. Patsy looks into the box, but she's still not sure to whom these things belong, nor what she's supposed to do with them. I cajole Patsy into the whelping box, but she won't lie down. Giving her the command to lie down, I facilitate the process by pushing down her butt. When her backend is finally down, I pull out her front legs. Like a seesaw, her backend goes up again. She knows exactly what she's doing. I can see a twinkle in her big eyes. Finally she lies down. I take the squirming puppies from the box one at a time and rub their noses against a nipple until they latch on. When all three are attached, I lie down on the sofa and watch. Patsy looks at me. "Oh," she seems to say, "this is good. I can do this." The babies's back feet push their bodies against their mommy's tummy while their front feet massage her large teats. Making sounds like the subdued wailing of distant sirens, they sleepily suck their mother's milk.

It's a quiet time, a sleepy time. Patsy has put her head down and shut her eyes. The flickering flame of the pellet stove dances against the darkness of early morning. Outside the rain beats against the windows and drums on the metal roof of the shed. The puppies continue nursing, gently slurping, slurping,

slurping.

Lying down on the sofa I wrap myself in the comfort of the sounds of nursing. How fortunate I am to be here in the warmth of this old house with Zoe and Melanie, the dogs, the puppies and the new babies. There is no other place in all the world I would rather be. Whatever the future holds, we'll meet it. Every ending is the birth of a new beginning.

More puppies to care for.

More puppies to love.

More laughter to fill our lives.

Epilogue

Bess's puppies, the ones we nurtured with loving care through the course of this book, now have grown up to be fine looking Newfoundlands. Mac (Mr. Orange) and Ros (Miss Red), who chose to live with us, are almost two, and the other puppies have found happy homes. Their new owners keep in touch with us, sending pictures of the puppies via e-mail. Mac is large, macho and laid back. When I'm picking up poop in the dog yard and stop to look at the woods across the river, Mac, as tall as I am, stands beside me on his hind legs, leaning on the fence. I put my arm around his shoulder and we watch the morning sun fill the woods with golden light. What a buddy. And he's still a loving lap dog, lying across my lap when I relax in the recliner.

Rosalind has turned into a svelte, graceful young lady. She's the nursemaid of the family. If Ellie is unhappy because another dog got her chewy, Ros bounds over to her and licks her eyes and ears. The other day when Zoe tripped on a rug, Ros was there to lick her face and comfort her. She's very intelligent and helps me when I'm working on various jobs around the house. I wouldn't be surprised if she picked up a hammer and went to work on a nail. Remember, she's the puppy who taught the other pups to use the dog door.

We kept one of the three puppies that were squirming after Patsy as the last chapter ended. Then he was only a pound and a half. Now he tips the scales at over 165 pounds. It seemed appropriate to name him Franklin since we already had an Eleanor. The other two puppies were sold to good homes. Franklin has a large head and expressive eyes like his mother. Already he's proven his virility by having sired seven puppies with one of Kathy Luce's ladies. We call him Goofball, because, as big as he is, he's still as playful as a puppy.

In the fall of 2004 our Empress Dowager, Jamielee, began to lose weight and was unable to process her food. When we took her to the vet, he ran several tests and did X-rays, but the results were inconclusive. Exploratory surgery was more than we wanted to put her through. He recommended that we feed her on a full protein diet in an attempt to get something into her system. Finally Zoe developed a new diet for her. She could have anything she wanted whenever she wanted it. Her favorite was peanut butter sandwiches. Knowing she might not be with us much longer, and with winter coming on, we prepared a grave in the orchard and covered it against the winter snow. Jamie managed to get through the winter and into the spring. She was still able to get down the steps to the river and Zoe took her for a swim each day the weather permitted.

The time came when she could no longer make it outdoors and it was clear to us that she was in pain. We took her to Angell Animal Medical Center in Springfield, and the resident internist came out to the van. As with Bear, Zoe held her in her arms as the doctor gave the shot. She died quietly. We brought her home and, with Martha's family and ours, buried her next to Bear and not far from little Kelly Green.

Last summer Bess had three more puppies, and a week later, Patsy had six. I set up two whelping boxes in the living room so one of us could watch over both sets of pups. For the next twelve weeks our house was filled with nine little comedians who kept us laughing.

Bess, our champion dog, was entered in the 2006 Westminster Dog Show in New York City, competing with the best Newfoundlands in the country. She's a natural born show dog and loves to be in the ring. Even though she didn't come in first, she made the final cut among the Newfoundlands. Zoe was there applauding her performance, while Melanie and I were at home taking care of our dog family.

As I finish this epilogue, we're between puppies and eagerly awaiting more. We're not the only ones. Mac and Franklin are strutting their stuff, eying the ladies and asking, "Okay, who's next."

Stay in touch with us through our web site. Melanie updates the log each Wednesday and it's filled with pictures of our dogs and all the puppies that are living with new families.

riverbearnewfoundlands.com

Rob Carpenter

Illustrator

Mac and Rob

Rob is a Summa Cum Laude BFA graduate of Hartford Art School at the University of Hartford. His paintings are hung in art collections throughout the United States. Rob's prints of Newfoundlands are routinely used as honors and prizes at large dog shows. The Newf Emporium is Rob's distributor for seven signed limited edition prints of Newfoundland dogs.

The illustrations in For The Love Of Puppies are cross-hatch ink drawings.

Prints of the art work in this book can be purchased as signed limited editions. For more information, please visit:

www.riverbearnewfoundlands.com/theartwork

Dan Montague

Dan and Ros

Dan Montague, onetime economic analyst with the CIA, Naval officer and Episcopal priest, retired as Director of Marketing for the Massachusetts Port Authority and began his writing career with the publishing of *White Wings* and *Second Chance*. He lives in western Massachusetts with his wife Zoë, daughter Melanie Carpenter and grandsons, Rob and McKey Carpenter.